With Angels Beside Us

With Angels Beside Us

Carmel Reilly

Constable & Robinson Ltd
3 The Lanchesters
162 Fulham Palace Road
London W6 9ER

www.constablerobinson.com

This edition published by Magpie Books,
an imprint of Constable & Robinson Ltd 2010

A copy of the British Library Cataloguing in
Publication Data is available from the British Library

ISBN 978-1-84901-550-9

Printed and bound in the EU

3 5 7 9 10 8 6 4 2

Contents

Introduction

A few years ago I edited a book called *Walking With Angels*. To research the book, I advertised asking for accounts of all sorts of meetings with angels. I was overwhelmed by the response I received to my request, and fascinated by the wide variety of accounts that arrived. In many cases, I had an interesting correspondence with the respondents as I tried to find out a little more about what had happened and how it had made them feel.

The experience of editing that book affected me strongly in a variety of ways. It is fascinating to see how people believe in angels and in the good they can do in the world. This is a faith that ranges across all creeds and ages, and it is hard to believe that this belief is without some foundation.

Most religions today do have some reference to angels. In the Christian tradition, angels have been seen as divine messengers, as part of the heavenly host, and as beings that originally shared the earth with people. In Judaism, Islam, Buddhism and Hinduism we also find stories and interpretations of angels. And it is not only those who adhere to a strict religious viewpoint who believe in angels – often we find that even those who are agnostic in their beliefs have found reason to believe that there are angels watching over us.

I have always tried not to let my own beliefs and faith affect how I approach the task of compiling these accounts. I suspect it is impossible truly to know the nature of angels. But also it seems that the best way for us to approach the truth is to compare and contrast as many different accounts of angelic nature as we are able to.

Following the publication of *Walking With Angels*, I have continued to receive a lot of correspondence regarding meetings with angels. As a result, I decided to compile some of these together with a number of accounts that I was not able to include in the first book. The result is this book.

Once again, I think it is intriguing to read the accounts that people feel compelled to share of their angelic encounters for two reasons. Firstly, we can discover a lot about angels from the information herein. Obviously, one has to read these accounts with a critical mind – in some cases the tellers of the stories are open about the fact that they are uncertain whether they met an angel or not.

In other cases they are convinced that they did meet an angel or receive assistance, but we may feel that there are more mundane explanations that could be employed. But given the weight of accounts we find here and elsewhere, it is hard to resist the idea that angels do exist and that we sometimes encounter them in our world.

The second reason I find these stories fascinating to compile is because of what they reveal about the people telling them. We see all kinds of people here, some in moments of crisis, some in emergencies and others in simple everyday settings. The minor details they tell us about their lives are testament to humanity's strengths and weaknesses, our capacity for both great kindness and cruelty.

If the angels do watch over us they must do so with a mixture of hope, frustration and love. We weave our lives into such tangled webs, yet we manage to find epiphanies in times of crisis, and love and joy in the darkest of times.

The Nature of Angels

I want to keep this introduction fairly brief, but I do think it is important to reiterate a few basic things we know from history and tradition about the nature of angels. The various religious sources tell us that angels are messengers from the world of pure spirit, and that they can be agents of divine intervention, and we also hear of guardian angels who watch over the lives of individuals. But what else do we know about them?

It is clear that angels are spiritual beings. But we also read that they are able to take on physical form sometimes. If we conceive of the physical and spiritual realm as separate aspects of the same universe, then we are bound to live in the physical world, with the ability to sometimes perceive pure spirit. Whereas the angels reside in the spiritual world and can sometimes manifest themselves in earthly form.

Medieval, renaissance and Victorian paintings often showed angels as winged creatures. This is in spite of the fact that there are very few references in scripture to angels having wings – they are more commonly described as taking human form.

In *Walking with Angels* I suggested that the reason for the imagery of wings derives from angels' role as messengers. The word 'angel' comes from the Greek *angelos*, (perhaps a translation of the Hebrew word *mal'akh*) meaning 'messenger'. This suggests that angels carry messages between the human world and other realms.

Since heaven was traditionally pictured as being above us, beyond the sky, it makes sense that angels were often seen as having wings with which they could traverse the spaces in between. However the more important part of this idea is that angels are messengers and that they provide a link between the physical world and the realm of pure spirit.

In accounts of meetings with angels we sometimes do find tales of winged creatures. But we also find examples where angels appear as people, as visions, as dream creatures or even as animals. Sometimes we find they are accompanied by white light, or by feelings of calm and joy, but there is no simple pattern.

Introduction

It doesn't seem unreasonable to assume that if angels are creatures of spirit, then they are able to choose how they manifest, and it might be that they know what earthly form is the one most likely to be recognised or to be of help to them in their mission.

Another common but questionable belief is that humans become angels when they die. This is an idea that has been explored at great length in fictional accounts of heaven. In religious texts it is more commonly suggested that angels are a separate class of being that predates humans, and that human spirits are a different thing again.

I don't want to apply a fixed view to this question. Some people do clearly believe that the spirits of their lost ones come back to them as angels. Whereas other accounts in this book seem to suggest that angels are quite different to people.

The final question I want to mention is that of why angels intervene in human existence. If one believes in God, then it is clear that angels are closer to God than ordinary mortals, so one must assume that angels can sometimes be acting as agents of divine will. But when one reads accounts of angels intervening in moments of emergency, to advise, warn or even save individuals from harm, then one has to wonder why they sometimes choose to act and sometimes abstain.

The best way I have found to imagine the relationship between angels and humans is to compare it to the relationship between adults and children. Humans have some understanding of the spiritual realm, but we are essentially bound by our physical form. When the angels perceive our struggles and endeavours, they perhaps see us as innocents, who are ignorant of many things that they know and who are in need of guidance and protection.

Just as an adult would feel an instinct to protect and instruct a child, perhaps the angels feel compelled to look after us. This would certainly be one way of understanding the many accounts we have where people feel that they have been in communication with their guardian angels.

Finally, I hope that this book will at the very least be thought provoking. The stories it contains tell us a great deal about the best and worst of humanity, while the interventions and messages of the angels give us reason to believe that there is a higher spiritual realm. No one can claim to have absolute knowledge of the angels (and if they did they would be a charlatan). But one can hope that the more we contemplate the angels and the spiritual realm, the more we come to understand what it is to be human.

Emergencies

Many accounts of experiences with angels come from situations of great danger. Whether we have guardian angels watching over us individually, or whether angels are more likely to reveal their presence when they are able to help people in an emergency is unclear. But what is certain is that many people are convinced that they have been helped out in their moment of need by the intervention of an angel.

Laura, 41

I'm a single mother. Anton's father left when he was just two years old, and we didn't have much contact afterwards, so it has always been just me and Anton. It is undoubtedly hard work being a parent on your own. You are constantly worrying about the things that could go wrong, accidents or risks, and you never really get a chance to turn off and stop being "on duty".

One lucky aspect of my life was that I always had a few good friends, and Jasmine, who has been there for me since we were teenagers, happened to have a lovely house out in the countryside near Lyon [in France]. So Anton and I did have some lovely holidays while he was growing up, which I wouldn't have been able to afford any other way.

I remember him when he was first learning to swim, with inflatable armbands and a rubber ring. I worried every time he went in the pool and always watched him like a hawk. In truth, those early holidays were not very relaxing for me.

He loved being in the pool and while Jasmine sometimes had friends over it would often be just me and Anton in the pool. So I had to be the lifeguard. Every time he got out of his depth I would feel anxious as I am not the world's strongest swimmer.

Finally he learned to swim. At first just easy widths in the shallow end, but gradually he became stronger and started being able to swim up and down to the deep end. Of course I kept worrying but I was proud of his progress and finally started being able to relax slightly when we were there together,

In the summer when he was eight I was there one day with Jasmine and a family she was friends with, who had two young children. I think Anton may have been showing off a bit as the children looked up to him, but it all seemed to be going well. I trusted him enough by this stage that I could read a book and lie on a sun lounger by the pool while he swam.

When the accident happened, the other family had taken their toddlers inside for a nap. Anton was happily splashing around in the shallow end on his own and I was absorbed in a book. Jasmine had also gone inside for some reason so it was just the two of us and for once I wasn't watching him.

Then I heard a voice very close to my ear saying "Look, now." It was the strangest thing, because there was no-one there and I had no reason to imagine anything was wrong. So I sat up and looked around and realised that I couldn't see Anton. I jumped up and saw that he was below the surface of the water, not moving.

The sense of panic I felt then still comes back to me when I think about it. I don't know if I could have lived with the guilt if he hadn't survived. I flung myself into the pool and grabbed for him, hauling him up first by one arm then with my arm around his chest. I have absolutely no memory of screaming, but Jasmine and the other two adults came running out as apparently I had let out a terrible shriek.

I dragged him over the edge of the pool where he lay

very still on his side, and immediately Jasmine took over while I scrabbled out. She knew exactly what to do, pumping his chest as he lay there, and then water came out of his mouth and he took in a terrible rasping breath. I started stroking his hair and talking to him and after a worrying moment or two he looked up. Thankfully it was soon clear that he hadn't suffered any terrible harm, though he could easily have drowned if he been in there any longer.

I didn't find out what had happened till later that night. He had been playing around, trying different ways of jumping into the water. The last experiment went wrong, and he had slipped on the wet stone just as he jumped.

He tried to get his head out of the way but it had glanced off the concrete edge of the pool and he must have blacked out for a moment. To me it would just have sounded like him jumping in as usual. The only reason I didn't sit there with my face stuck in a book for another few minutes before looking up was that strange voice I heard in my head.

I must admit I spent the rest of his childhood and teenage years worrying that something like that would happen again and he often used to tell me off for worrying too much and fussing over him. What he didn't understand was that I felt blessed to still have him, not to have lost him because of that one little slip and a moment when I wasn't concentrating on him. But thankfully he has now safely grown to be a strong young man, perfectly able to look after himself. I can be proud of him, as his mother, I always will be, but I know that I owe his life to whatever force was looking after him that day.

Karl, 40

Back in 2001, my whole family went into London to do some shopping. We took the underground train to Oxford Circus and because it was a Saturday afternoon, it was very crowded. My youngest son, Miles, was carrying Ed, his favourite teddy bear. He never went anywhere without him. As we pushed forward to get off the train, Miles dropped his bear and went back inside to get him. At that moment the doors of the tube train closed and the train drove off.

My wife and I just panicked and ran after the train waving our arms. The train didn't stop. It disappeared into the tunnel. We immediately called the guard and told him what had happened, the guard said that he would radio through and get someone to bring our son back. Our daughter, Louise, was very upset at what had happened to her little brother and kept asking when we would see him again.

The guard led us through to the platform where the trains went the opposite way and told us to wait. Eventually a train came in but Miles wasn't on it. The guard looked puzzled and we went to the platform where we'd originally been standing.

As the crowd thinned out we could see Miles standing

on the platform holding Ed. We rushed to him and asked him what had happened. He told us that the train was going the wrong way and a nice man had helped him to get back here. He told us that they had flown. The guard was mystified because the train was now at the next station and the platform had been empty a few moments before.

A few years later, Miles was diagnosed with Hodgkin's Disease and spent a lot of time in hospital. Thankfully, he did recover but kept telling us that the nice man from the train was visiting him at night.

Angela, 45

Back in 1969, when I was about five years old, I was at home with my Auntie Ellen. My mother and father were out for the evening and Auntie Ellen had come to babysit. I was playing with a bowl of pebbles that we'd collected the last time we went to the beach and Auntie Ellen was fixing up some food for us in the kitchen. I'm not sure what happened next but I must have accidentally swallowed one, I remember choking and trying to cough the pebble out but it seemed to go further down my throat.

I was making quite a racket and Auntie Ellen came running into the room and banged frantically on my back at the same time as calling for an ambulance. I think at one point she even held me upside down and shook me.

I remember floating outside my body, looking down at Auntie Ellen as she tried to dislodge the pebble. I could see her working frantically to save me. I turned and noticed something hovering to my right. There was a beautiful woman floating next to me, she was wearing a sort of long dress in shades of vivid blue, red and green, very bright and it flowed around her as if she was in water.

She smiled at me and I felt so peaceful. I had no idea who she could be back then but now I know she was an angel sent to me by God. She told me that it was not my time yet and even though I was just a little girl, I knew what she meant.

Suddenly I coughed and was back with Auntie Ellen. She was holding me and I wasn't choking any more. She had finally dislodged the stone. My throat was pretty sore and I was taken into hospital overnight for observation. Auntie Ellen told me years later that she was terrified that I'd died because my lips turned blue and I didn't seem to be breathing. I told her about the lady I had seen with me and she said that it must be an angel.

Willem, 78

My father was in the German army during the Second World War. Some people may take the view that in a war there are good guys and bad guys, and that anyone on the German side in that war was a bad guy. But I cannot believe that God or the angels look down and make judgments that are so simple. Of course, the people who made the war happen, the people who set up death camps – it is hard to see them as anything other than evil. But many of the people who did the fighting were simply innocent young men who felt they had to fight for their country. If we could just find out how to stop young men being prepared to follow their terrible leaders into war or acts of terror then we might be able to live in a world without war, but I think that is a long way away from us now. Possibly even further away than it was when I was a young man.

Certainly, my father was very distressed after the war when he found out the extent of the things that had happened. He had been only a teenager when he joined the army. He was often sad and depressed in later life, but at the same time he was determined to make a good life for his wife and family, and I'm lucky to be able to say that he succeeded. My home life was a happy one and the things I know about his time in the war were things he only told me when I was old enough to understand them.

Anyway, the particular incident I want to tell you about happened to him while he was fighting in the North East of France, late in the war, when the German army was on the back foot. He was a good distance from the front. He was mainly involved in maintaining supply lines. He was in a village in a fairly calm area, and there was no reason to expect any attack although, of course, there were always precautions that were sensible in wartime.

My father was simply walking through the village on that day with two of his colleagues, when he heard a woman's voice behind him clearly calling him by his name. He told me later that it sounded like someone he knew, but he couldn't say exactly who. He was surprised as the villagers didn't speak to them much and of course he had no female colleagues in the village. So he hesitated, and told his colleagues to wait a moment while he turned back – neither of them had heard anything.

As he turned his back there was an explosion about twenty yards away, exactly where he would have been if he had kept walking. He was thrown off his feet and his two colleagues, who had turned to watch him, were too. But none of them were seriously injured. Clearly, it had been a trap set for them by resistance fighters, and they were lucky to escape with their lives.

His feeling was that something had saved his life in that moment, and he called it an angel. But when he told me about it he also questioned why an angel would choose to save him. After all, so many other people died – his friends included. Good people on all sides died in the war and, perhaps, he was saved.

I can't really explain, but perhaps there is only so much that angels can do to save people in such terrible times. What I do know is that if an angel chose to save him, then they did so because he was a good man, not because of what his uniform represented.

June, 37

Years ago, during a week-long stay in hospital, I had a strange experience. I had drifted off to sleep at night and suddenly woke up. I was freezing. There was a woman kneeling by my bed and the room had a white mist swirling around it.

Suddenly, the woman grabbed my arm and pulled me so that I had to look at her. She whispered to me that I had to keep strong and not give up. I had been suffering from liver disease and was feeling very weak. The old woman insisted that I needed to get better.

I eventually went back to sleep and, when I woke up the next morning, presumed that I had had a bad dream However, when I looked at my arm it was ringed with bruises as if someone had been holding it very tightly. My liver regained some sort of balance and I recovered. The day after I left hospital I discovered I was pregnant. I think that this is why the old woman wanted me to stay alive.

Brenda, 45

One weekend my husband and I went sailing with another couple who we were friendly with. We agreed to take it slowly because my husband had been rushed to hospital the previous month with a suspected minor heart attack.

We had brought a picnic and were all in a very jolly mood as we pulled away from the dock. It was a lovely peaceful afternoon and after about three hours we decided to sail back to shore.

We got quite near to the dock when suddenly the boat tipped sideways and began to capsize. We all scrambled to get out of the boat before it turned over completely. As I struggled, my skirt became stuck on a broken bit of wood and I couldn't get free. I was in danger of being badly injured or killed because the propeller was only a few inches from me and I was slipping. I can't swim and was very frightened.

I screamed at the others to help me and saw a man's arm come through the water and pull me clear of the broken wood. As I got to the surface I saw my husband and friends swimming to the dock. In their rush they hadn't thought to look for me as they presumed I was following them.

I was wondering who could have helped me. I still felt as if I was being held above water and it was strange because I wasn't even trying to swim. I looked down and realised that somehow one of the lifejackets from the boat had got under my body. I didn't remember grabbing it. As I made my way to the dock and climbed out, I once again got that lifting feeling and managed to climb onto the dock with minimum fuss.

My husband and friends looked at the life jacket in astonishment. Apparently, they had been locked in the cabin because the boat owner had had some problems with theft. I didn't have the key and I didn't know where they were.

I can only assume that whatever lifted me clear of the boat and got me safely to shore must have also given me a life vest. I can't think that it could be anything other than an angel.

Tanya, 20

I had a heart transplant when I was twenty months old. I have to be really careful with illnesses because my immune system is compromised and I can become seriously ill very quickly. When I was eleven, I got a bout of flu that turned into pneumonia and I was hospitalised. I was so ill that doctors were worried that I might die. I was in a coma for a few days and as I regained consciousness I kept feeling as if someone was standing by my bed leaning in close to me.

I opened my eyes and could see mom talking to a nurse in the corner of the room, so it couldn't have been her. On the other side of me I could sense that there was someone there. When I turned my head I saw that it was a man with a beautiful and kind face wearing all white, who told me that it was time for me to wake up. Over the next few days he came to my bedside quite often.

As my health improved I told my mother about the man and she asked the doctors who he might be but they insisted that only the doctors who treated me and two other nurses came to my bedside and they had no idea who it could be. I think it was an angel looking after me. He told me to wake up because it wasn't my time yet.

Celia, 45

My grandfather was caught up in an earthquake in the 1930s in Greece. He was in his house when the worst shock arrived and it basically collapsed around him.

He had managed to get himself under a table, and once the dust settled he found himself trapped in a tiny space, not even big enough to stretch out. There was dust everywhere and he was choked by it for a while. He also had no water.

Large chunks of the building were pinning the table down, and he was unable to move the brickwork around him. So the only thing he could do was to sit tight and pray that someone would find him.

He told me that the first few hours were terrible, as he couldn't hear any movement outside, and there was a series of tremors which could easily have shifted the masonry above him and crushed him. For all he knew, everyone had died out there. He yelled for a long time for help, but he didn't get any response.

He just lay curled up in that tiny space, praying. He was desperately thirsty and worried about whether he had enough air.

He told me that after a while he heard a voice in his ear telling him that help was on the way and not to give up. He was really scared that he wasn't going to make it, but the voice in his ear told him not to panic and to shout again. So he yelled as loud as he could. He said it was really hard because his throat was parched. But he yelled and also banged a rock against the ground to try and attract attention.

And then finally he started to hear distant tapping. All the while that the rescuers were coming, he kept shouting from time to time, and tapping the rock so they wouldn't give up. And all the time he heard that voice in his ear telling him that it was going to be OK.

When he was pulled out of the ruins, he was shocked by the devastation he found around him – and deeply grateful both to his rescuers and to that voice in his ear that had kept him going at the darkest moment.

Beth, 20

When I was eleven years old I had a dream one cold winter about my little brother who had passed away four years earlier in a boating accident. In my dream he came to visit me at school. He didn't go to my school when he was alive as he was too young. In the dream I could see him standing on the edge of the playing fields where the grass slopes down into the lane.

In winter we had had lots of fun riding down the snowy slopes at the side of the school field. However, in this particular dream my brother was standing silently by the slope, holding the hand of an angel. He seemed very distant and when I shouted at him to come and join me he shook his head and pointed into the distance. I was crying when I woke up because the dream had brought back to me how much I loved and missed my little brother. It was a cold, clear, sunny day as I walked to school, perfect for sliding. I planned to slide with some friends at lunchtime.

When the bell went for lunch we were a bit late getting to the fields because I was telling them about my dream. Suddenly things began to happen very quickly. A road gritting truck was coming down the lane when it started to skid. As the driver tried to correct the skid the truck crashed into the slope at the side of field, exactly where we intended to play. If we had got there earlier we may have all been killed. My brother had been warning me of the danger.

Jim, 56

I was helped by an angel once when I got lost in an October blizzard.

I was staying with friends in Canada, and I had driven into town to pick up some groceries. The town was about five miles from where they lived in a small community, and there wasn't much inbetween except the road, some woodland and the prairie.

While I was there, I stopped in at the cinema to watch a movie. When I came out I discovered that there was some heavy snow falling. This had been predicted but we were expecting it later in the night so I was taken by surprise. I put the groceries into the car and set off driving cautiously along the road.

To start with I was fine as I could see the side of the road and the snow wasn't too deep. I had to go slowly, but I was making progress. But then the snow got really heavy and I started to find it hard to see where the road was. I was crawling along, and there was no other traffic on that road, so I had nothing to give me a clue where I should be pointing the car. All I could see was white and the swirling snow as it fell more heavily.

I had more or less decided to give up and head back to town when I skidded. I was going slowly so while it was alarming, it wasn't too much of a problem, except that the car went off the road and slid down a gentle slope onto the edge of a field. I could get it restarted, but it simply wouldn't drive back up that little slope to the road, it just kept falling back into the field.

I had three choices – head back to town, stay in the car and hope for help from passers by, or head on to my friends' house. The last choice seemed the worst as I thought I was less than half way there. But I thought I might freeze if I stayed in the car. I could see the lights from the town very dimly back down the road, so I decided to head that way.

I had some good boots and a very warm coat, but still it was extremely cold out there. I started trudging down that road, struggling to keep my feet in the icy snow. The town didn't seem to be getting any closer, but I figured if I kept on going I'd make it in the end.

Then I found myself facing a barbed wire fence. I had been sure I was following the road, but it turned out that I had left it behind somehow and was in a snow-covered field.

I couldn't get through the barbed wire at that point and I couldn't retrace my steps, so I followed the fence along for about ten minutes till I found a gate, then I went through. I thought if I follow the fence it might mean I stayed safe, but then I thought I saw the lights of the town again, so I headed off away from the fence into the deep snow of the field.

It must have been a trick of the light, though, because I lost sight of the lights and the fence and now I didn't have a clue where I was going. I couldn't stop where I was, so I had to just keep going and pray I found someone. I started to remember stories about people dying in the snow, and about those who had survived by digging themselves into snowy drifts. Or had they died because they tried to do that? I couldn't remember, but I was getting seriously worried.

At that point I heard a voice calling me. It was saying, "This way."

Of course, I headed straight towards the voice, desperate to find someone who could help me out. I kept following that voice, but however hard I tried to catch up with it I couldn't find the person. But it kept calling me "this way", and "keep going", and I kept on walking towards it.

Then, all of a sudden, I saw real lights in front of me, at first quite faint, but then bright enough that I believed they were real. It was a farmhouse.

I banged on the door and an old couple came and answered it together. They were amazed to see me, apparently they were pretty much on the edge of the prairie and if I had missed their house I could have walked all night and most of the next day without finding another building. I was heading more or less straight away from the town, so my navigation had been atrocious.

I thanked the old man for saving me but he didn't know what I was talking about. I said that I had only found their house because he had called me. He told me that he and his wife had been sitting reading in the parlor and there was no-one else there, or within a mile or so of the house.

I didn't believe him to start with. But then he looked at me and said that if that had happened to him, he'd be thanking his guardian angel. I don't know if that is what saved me or not, but I do know I'd have frozen to death that night if I'd kept on making my own decisions about which way to walk.

Suzanna, 29

I've always been pretty sceptical about the supernatural because I think I am a fairly logical person. However, when I had a serious accident there were some events that left me wondering.

One night in 2007, I had a very serious car crash in which the car was completely written off. All I remember about the accident is the moment when I knew there would be an impact and the world seemed to be in slow motion. I had a head-on collision with a car that was coming in the opposite direction.

He was overtaking and didn't get time to pull out of my way. I saw that the car was going to hit me and then I remember my car being spun round and hitting my head hard against the driver's window. I could hear the crunch of metal as I spun. Strangely enough, I didn't feel any fear.

I suddenly became aware that there was a man sitting next to me. He was holding the back of my head to stop me hitting it again and as the car came to a stop I realised that I was going to be alright. I didn't question where my other passenger had come from.

Once everything had gone still and silent I turned to the man next to me to thank him. There was no one there. So, even through my scepticism I think something supernatural happened that day. An angel saved me.

Constantine, 64

When I was a child in Greece, we used to stop and pay our respects to the shrines by the road. My grandmother always told me that the angels look after us, even if we don't know about it at the time.

When I was about fourteen, I was with my grandmother walking towards the next village along, when a wall beside the road simply collapsed. It had perhaps been weakened in a storm or by erosion of the soil at the base, but without warning it fell towards us. I grabbed my grandmother's arm and tried to pull her with me but she was closer to the wall and a section of it fell on to her leg.

When the dust settled, I realised that she was pinned to the ground by this heavy section of wall. I couldn't tell how bad the injury was. She was awake, though very shocked and clearly in considerable pain.

I knew there was a doctor in the nearby town and that the sooner we got her there, the more chance she would have. I tried to lift the wall from her leg but it was so heavy I couldn't shift it.

I was terrified but determined not to give up, so I braced myself and lifted as hard as I could. I shouted at my grandmother to move but she didn't respond. I'm not sure if she couldn't or didn't understand.

At this point I was in trouble. I was like a weightlifter trying to support more weight than I was capable of, and I was about to drop it. I knew that I had probably been rash to rush in so quickly and now I was in danger of dropping the wall back on to her leg and making any injury worse.

I remember praying for someone to help me. I was desperate. And then from somewhere I felt a big push, lifting the wall that tiny bit higher so that with one more huge effort I was able to throw it clear of her leg. I swear I could not have done that on my own, so I am convinced I had some help from an angel or from God himself.

My grandmother was not light but I managed to hoist her up and carry her to the next village where there was a man with a car. He took us to the doctor. My grandmother had a broken leg but he was able to set it so that she recovered in good time.

I did tell her about the angel afterwards. She wanted to give me all the credit for helping her, but I felt I needed to be honest that I had nearly made a mess of everything and things had only turned out for the best because I got some extra help.

Jason, 45

In the 1980s, I worked for a postal company. There was one road where I always had a delivery every month. It was to a house that had an elderly couple living in it who seemed to do all their shopping by mail order. Their address was only a short walk from my apartment block so I always saved that delivery until last so that I could then go straight home.

The road home was a narrow two-lane street without a pavement. The usual rule was to walk on the side of the road facing oncoming traffic so you could see any danger in advance. I had a strange experience as I was walking home one night. I heard a voice in my ear telling me to get off the road as quickly as possible. I'm not generally the sort of person who hears voices and for a moment wondered what was going on.

Then I heard the loud rasping of a car engine and a car careened round the bend in the road heading straight for me. I couldn't work out how I had been warned and so felt very confused. At that precise moment, I felt myself being lifted off the road and flung into the grass verge beside the hedge. The car skidded over exactly where I'd been standing and I realised that if I hadn't moved it would probably have killed me.

The car itself skidded back over to the other side of the road and ran up onto the grass verge. I went over to the car and found that the driver was a teenage boy who was clearly under the influence of drugs, alcohol or maybe both. I knew that there was a phone booth just around the corner so I went and called the emergency services. When they came, the paramedics had to resuscitate the boy. I later found out that he'd taken what could possibly have been an overdose of heroin.

Sometime later, I had a call from his parents thanking me for saving his life. I assured them that I'd only done what anyone would have done but I always wonder about that night. Was there an angel looking after both me and the boy? Certainly two lives were saved where both could very easily have lost.

Mario, 57

My stepfather was quite a violent man. He moved in with my mother when I was four and things were never quite right at home when he was there. We were all terrified of him. I think he drank too much and that made him an unpredictable man. I remember seeing him throw a brick through the neighbours' window once. At the time it seemed funny, but now it seems a rather grim memory.

Of course, when I was a kid it was OK to punish children physically. It was fairly normal to hit them if they had done something wrong. I didn't think I had any right to complain. But looking back I think he went too far. We would get punished for the tiniest things, and he would really hurt us when he hit us. In the end my mother kicked him out, after he started hitting her, too but for a few years it was a bad time in our house.

It's a horrible feeling when you have been punished and don't feel like you deserve it. I used to try and find a dark little corner to go and hide in afterwards. It was partly a place to lick my wounds, to stay still while my hands or legs were stinging from being slapped. But it was also a cocoon, a place where I could be completely alone and imagine being somewhere completely different.

I remember the wardrobe in my sister's room was a place I often went. She was away working as she was ten years older than me. Later she told me she moved away to get away from him.

Her wardrobe had a nice calm smell and I could burrow right to the back of it, pushing her old shoes out of the way and pulling the coats around me so I was almost invisible.

If there was an angel in there with me they never talked to me. But I do remember several times when I felt these warm strong arms coming round me in the dark. I could feel them very clearly and I could feel something like breath on my face.

I've always believed I had no-one I could depend on except myself, and I am not a religious person. So in some ways I'm not sure about how I feel about that memory. But at the time I really felt it was an angel in there comforting me and it made me feel warm and strong again. Maybe I was young enough to be open to ideas that I've since closed my mind to.

Peter, 62

I used to be a policeman and back in the 1980s I was involved in a high speed chase. I was driving round a bend in the road when I hit what felt like black ice. The car began skidding out of control and as I struggled to regain control of the car I suddenly had a realisation that no matter what I did I couldn't get the car to stay on the road.

At this point I took my feet of the pedals, put my arms over my head and let go of the steering wheel. I was trying to protect my head from going through the windscreen when I finally crashed into something.

Suddenly there was a loud crunch sound and I could feel the police car starting to turn over. I took my arms away and grabbed the steering wheel to have something to hold onto if we rolled and suddenly the car rocked back and coasted round the curve in the road.

The suspect I was chasing had crashed into roadside barriers after hitting another patch of ice on the road. When I got out of the car to arrest him he looked stunned. In his statement later he said that something seemed to grab his car and throw it into the barriers.

I also felt that our experience on that road was weird. There were no skid marks on any bit of the road and on closer examination there was no ice either. I don't know what happened on that road but I think an angel was watching me that day.

Andre, 28

The time when I was helped by an angel was when I was badly injured in a fire. It was in this house party I went to. I wasn't feeling very well, after a late night the day before, and I had had a few drinks, so I'd gone up to the top floor to lie down for a while. I found a warm armchair in a room, and I fell asleep there which is one reason I got caught up in the fire.

I was woken by a man shaking my shoulder. He was about fifty, with a lined face and pale blue eyes. I smelt acrid smoke and saw flames flickering through the window. What had happened was that someone had knocked a candle over and the fire spread pretty quickly from the ground floor to the staircase. Almost everyone had managed to get out straight away, as the front and back doors were clear and it took the fire a while to reach the stairs. But no-one had realised I was upstairs, so I was left behind.

I was pretty panicky. I wasn't sure where the man who had woken me had gone, but when I opened the door I soon realised that I was trapped. It was intensely hot and as soon as I opened the door, flames shot towards me, scorching my arms. I ran back into the room I had been in and slammed the door behind me. There was only one window, but I knew I had to jump. I pulled it open, with difficulty, and looked out.

It was pretty scary. The flames I had seen were coming out of the windows downstairs and there was smoke billowing around everywhere. But I could see a shed roof which I thought I could reach, so I just flung myself towards it. I just managed to reach it, though I slithered off and fell onto the grass below. A group of people quickly surrounded me and pulled me away from the house down the garden.

I was lucky really. I had some nasty burns down one side, some bad bruises and a broken rib and wrist. Overall, it was extremely painful but I could have been far worse.

I was conscious in the ambulance that took me to the hospital, but once I was there I was sedated, and I woke up in a bed with casts and bandages all over me. The man who had saved me by shaking my shoulder was sitting in the chair. He smiled and went out of the room, then my father came in and started telling me what an idiot I was for nearly dying.

I was there for a few days and I saw the man two more times, but never when anyone else was around. I asked the nurses about him, but none of them had seen him so they couldn't tell me anything about him. I'm pretty sure that no-one else could see him because he was an angel.

Alexis, 57

I grew up in Jamaica. When I was young I used to be out in the boat fishing a lot, but this is a story that my granddad told me.

He was out one day when a storm blew up. His boat was quite rickety and the engine failed. He was fishing just off a rocky part of the coast and the wind started to drive him towards the rocks.

He fought to keep the boat away, and tried hard to get the engine going again, but it was refusing to start and he was in danger of being thrown on to the rocks together with his boat, So the safest thing he could do was to abandon his boat.

He dived into the rough water and started to try and swim around towards the part of the coast where there was a beach. He was a strong swimmer but this was treacherous water and he was still in danger of ending up on the rocks. He heard his boat hitting the rocks and starting to be smashed, but he just had to keep swimming away. He was having to swim out to sea just to try and get out of the current that was pushing him towards the rocks.

He kept swimming and reached deeper water where he was able to turn and head back towards the shallows of the beach. But he was starting to tire and was worried that he might not make it.

He told me that as he swam he said a prayer in his head over and over, "Lord Jesus, have mercy on me." He used this prayer to try and keep him going as he weakened, and he kept thinking about my grandmother and my aunts and uncles, who were young children at the time.

The storm was getting worse, so it got harder. He didn't know how long he was out there, but it seemed like a very long time.

At a certain point he started to lose the will to keep going. And at this stage he heard a voice beside him urging him to keep going. He felt that it was in response to his prayers. The voice told him that he would make it to the shore if he just kept moving his arms and legs and that no matter how tired he was, he had to keep going. It told him he would see his family again.

With this voice in his ear, he found a new strength and started to manage to make some real headway. Eventually, he found he was getting closer to the beach instead of further away, and then finally he hauled himself up on to the sand.

He told me he cried with relief when he felt solid land under him and said another prayer of thanks. And at that moment he heard the voice one more time, congratulating him, but telling him that he should remember how he had been saved and not waste the second chance he had been given.

He rolled over on to his back and thanked the voice and, if you believe him, he always remembered that he owed his life to an angel and tried to live as good a life as he could. He wasn't a perfect man, but he certainly always looked out for us all and he was someone that anyone could go to for help in difficult times, so I think he really did do his best.

David, 35

My cousin Steven was always obsessed with motorcycles. He passed his road test first time and bought himself a 600cc bike. It was second-hand but he spent hours reconditioning it and polishing it. Once he had tuned the engine and replaced the tyres, he decided that he would take it for a spin on the local highway.

He said later that he got the bike up to 75mph on a fairly empty road. However, he was so excited to be riding fast on his new bike that he missed his turning off the road and sped past it. He knew that the next turn off was fifteen miles along and for some stupid reason he decided to do a u-turn in the middle of the highway.

He slowed down, but still misjudged how fast he could do the turn. As he attempted to turn, he was still going at such a speed that his bike skidded and he could feel that he was going to hit the ground at speed.

The next thing he was aware of was that there was another biker with him, holding his head and keeping him still on the ground. The man with him talked calmly and told him that help was coming. Steven said that he thought he had passed out once or twice but each time the man with him struggled to keep him conscious by talking to him and reassuring him.

Eventually he could hear the sirens of the emergency vehicles and see their lights in the distance. The paramedics got him into the ambulance and the next thing he knew was waking up in a hospital bed.

Steven enquired about the man who had helped him as he lay on the road but was told that he had been alone and that the person who called them about his accident had been a truck driver travelling in the opposite direction.

We have all since wondered if there could have been a motorbiking angel looking out for him that night.

Carolyn, 52

There was an angel in the room when I was told that I had breast cancer.

I had found a lump one day and had of course gone to the doctor. They had done some tests and I had to go back to find out what had happened. I was very scared on the way there. I had been having sleepless nights worrying about what was going to happen.

Cancer is such a big word and of course it covers a lot of different problems, some of which are far worse than others. But I was frightened. I sat there in the waiting room biting my nails and getting stressed every time someone's name was called.

Finally I was invited into the doctor's surgery. When I got to the room, he told me he had to go and fetch my files. He left the room for a moment and when he closed the door I saw that there was a woman sitting behind it. I was a bit shocked as I thought it was a junior assistant or something. But she came over and held my hand and told me not to be scared. Then she left the room, just before the doctor came back.

I asked her who she had been and he just looked at me as though I was mad. He told me no-one had been there. I didn't argue because I realised something strange was happening.

He gave me the diagnosis and I did have cancer. But he assured me that they were going to be able to do something about it, and that it was operable if we moved quickly.

Having been so scared for the whole week beforehand, I found myself ridiculously calm now. I almost ended up having to assure the doctor, to tell him it was all going to work out for the best. I think he was a bit startled since I had arrived looking pale and panicky, but what the woman had said to me had made all the difference.

Afterwards I went out to the car and drove off. As I left the car park, I saw the woman on the other side of the road. She gave me a big smile and waved and then turned a corner and I never saw her again.

It turned out fine, just as she had said. I had to have a part of my breast removed, but compared to what some people go through I have to feel lucky. I am very conscious that many people have far worse problems, so I have always tried to be positive about it. But I am grateful to the woman, who I believe was an angel, for helping me to calm down when I first received the bad news.

A lot of people have told me that it makes a big difference if you can stay calm rather than getting stressed and I can only think that her intervention was the best thing that could possibly have happened to me at that moment.

Caroline, 54

I suffer from tinnitus and also from an excessive sensitivity to noise.

Recently I had a terrible problem with one of my neighbours. He kept having parties and playing thumping music into the small hours. I was close to having a nervous breakdown over it. I asked him repeatedly to be more considerate but he was just one of those people who didn't care. As far as he was concerned his right to enjoy his music was of equal or greater importance than my right to peaceful enjoyment of my own home. It didn't occur to him that as soon as he played music at that volume, he was actually intruding into my home and thus behaving completely unreasonably.

One night I came close to the end of my tether. I had been happily getting ready for bed at about eleven o'clock, when he came home with a group of people and put on his music at the loudest I could ever remember. They were shouting and singing along, and it felt like something they were doing deliberately to upset me. Of course, I know it wasn't as personal as that, they were just selfish rather than deliberately attacking me, but the problem with these kinds of issues is that you lose sight of common sense.

So I roamed around my house, trying to read, watch TV or somehow find a way to shut up the consciousness of this dreadful noise, but nothing helped and I just gradually became more and more distressed.

At about three in the morning, I started crawling around on my floor, punching cushions and the sofa to take out the anger I felt at the way he was behaving. I knew there was absolutely no point in going round to complain.

I looked up from the floor and found that an angel was standing there in the room with me. She spread her arms and looked at me. I got up and she gave me a big hug. It was the most glorious feeling – it was as though warmth and light were spreading right through me.

Then she led me to bed, and put a finger on her lips. As she did that, the noise abruptly stopped. I have no idea why, but I couldn't help feeling she had somehow taken pity on me and helped me.

I fell asleep almost as soon as I hit the pillow. For whatever reason, that was the worst problem I had and for a long while after that, the noise improved. There were occasional moments when the noise upset me, but I never got to the same state of distress.

These days I live out in the countryside. It suits me much better than a town. My nearest neighbour is half a mile away and I am more likely to be woken up by foxes or owls than by a neighbour's sound system.

Tom, 51

I believe I was helped by an angel once when I hurt my leg. I was on a long walk on the North Devon coast, on my own. I had wandered away from the footpath to take a closer look at some of the rock formations. It was on a steep slope with scree underfoot, and I lost my footing. I slid down the slope into a little gully, landing hard on my left foot.

I knew immediately I'd broken something. I still thought I'd be OK because I wasn't that far from the path, so I thought I could either shout for help or crawl back there.

I tried crawling first. It was extremely painful and I soon realised it was a very difficult task. I couldn't put any weight at all on the foot and it was going to be impossible to get up the slope without doing so. The other directions were not promising at all as they led in jagged rocks which I wouldn't be able to get across.

I checked my mobile phone of course, but there was no signal at all. So I started shouting. I called and called, for what seemed like hours but no one was coming. The wind was pretty strong and I was close to the sea and I can imagine the sound was just getting lost. Also there was only likely to be a few walkers an hour along that path and I couldn't be sure when they were likely to be closest.

I had a little bit of water in a bottle, but not a great deal. And while the weather was pleasant enough in the day, I definitely didn't want to spend the night exposed to the elements. I was starting to panic when I saw a woman standing above me. She looked to be about my age, and I've never been so pleased to see someone in my life. She waved at me. I shouted to her that I needed help. She just smiled and waved, then walked back so I couldn't see her any more.

At the time I had a really strange feeling about her. The sunlight had been coming from behind her and she seemed almost to be giving off a light of her own. And the calm way she reacted to me was also peculiar. I didn't know what to think.

For a few moments I thought maybe she was mad and I had been incredibly unlucky to be found by her. Then two men appeared at the top of the slope. They scrambled down to where I was lying and told me that a woman had told them that I was hurt and needed help. She had stayed at the path.

They helped me up the slope. With two of them working together it was not too difficult, they more or less carried me up there. I would say it took five minutes, no more.

When we got to the top the woman wasn't visible anywhere. I suppose I thought that she must have walked on once she had found help for me. Once we were up there, they helped me along the path to a point where the road was about half a mile away across a field, and they helped me across. Then one of them walked to the nearest house to call an ambulance while I sat on the verge with the other man.

I had broken my left ankle, and it had to be set. I took the phone numbers of the two men who had helped me and sent them flowers afterwards to thank them for their help. I'm actually still in touch with them both as they live in my area.

But I never saw the woman again. I started to believe she was an angel when I eventually revisited the scene of my accident, the following year. I found the exact place on the path, and walked over to the edge of the gully I had been stuck in (very carefully!)

The visibility at that point was excellent. You could see about a mile along the path in both directions. But it had only taken us five minutes to scramble up the slope. She wouldn't have been out of sight in any direction. I don't see how she could simply have disappeared in that amount of time, and right from the start I had had a strange feeling when I saw her. I'll never know for sure, but if anyone asks me I am happy to tell them that I believe she was an angel who came to help me when I needed it most.

Kayla, 37

I had a pretty wild childhood. I was in and out of trouble at home, I dabbled with drugs and I hung around with some people who I would have been better avoiding. When I was sixteen my mother threw me out of the house after a huge argument, so I got on a train to Chicago.

I didn't know anyone in the city and I only had a few hundred dollars in my pocket. I found a cheap room and looked for work, but I didn't look hard enough, or wasn't lucky enough to get a job and soon my money was running out. When I had twenty dollars left, I packed my little bag and left the room I was in. It was summer and I thought I would be able to find somewhere to sleep.

The first night I was homeless was awful. I was terrified and couldn't find anywhere that seemed safe. Places like parks and back alleys that seem like somewhere you could hide in the daylight turn into a kind of scary jungle at night and every sound you hear seems like it must be someone who is going to attack or rob you.

Next day I was walking round in a daze when this man in a sports car came crawling along the road beside me. He thought I was a prostitute. At first I ignored him. This had happened to me before and I found it disgusting. But he was persistent and suddenly I thought about how little money I had. I talked to him and he offered me $100, which would have made a big difference to me.

So, even though I knew it was wrong I got into the car and went back to his apartment. He took me to the bedroom and went off to the bathroom.

I sat there feeling numb and scared about what was going to happen next. I had never slept with anyone, so I had no idea what I was doing. It was moment of real desperation.

Then I closed my eyes and I saw this angel. It was

exactly like the stone angels in the church my grandma used to take me to as a kid, but it was alive and breathing. It had this very stern expression on its face, quite awesome and terrifying. It managed to combine sadness with anger.

I opened my eyes and thought very hard for a moment, then I knew that the angel was right. I was taking a wrong turn and it would be something I would always regret.

I grabbed my coat and ran out of the apartment before the man could come back out. I ran and ran in case he tried to come after me in his car. After a few blocks, I couldn't run any more. I found myself outside a church, so I went in.

I knelt and tried to pray, to ask for guidance. I couldn't see that angel's face any more but I remembered exactly how it had looked.

At that moment the priest came to talk to me. I was obviously looking pretty rough and scared, and he was worried. I poured my heart out to him, told him everything. I even told him about how close I had come to being a prostitute.

At first his face was a little like the angel's. He looked sad, too and, if not angry, stern. He was a good man. He managed to find a hostel where I could stay for a week. It was basic but clean. And while I was there he also took me to a local restaurant where they needed someone to wash dishes. They weren't sure to start with as I looked so young, but he vouched for me and they gave me a chance.

I won't say everything in my life went smoothly after that. Let's just say I never make things easy for myself! But getting that job and a place to stay got me back on my feet at that stage so I will always be grateful to that man. And while I have had a few strange times in my life I have never again stooped as low as I did that day, so seeing that angel at that exact moment definitely made a real difference to my life.

Tom, 56

About eight years ago I was skiing in the French Alps during an exceptionally cold winter. I didn't really mind because I went skiing every year and I loved it. On this particular day, I started out very early in the morning.

I did two runs on the slope and then began to feel very strange. Then I heard a voice in my head saying, "Hospital." Suddenly, there was a pain across my chest and I was worried that I was having a heart attack.

I decided that I would get to my chalet and then telephone for help. I was quite a way away from where I was staying but there were very few people around and my French isn't too good.

By the time I reached my chalet I was exhausted and immediately collapsed on the floor. Suddenly, a voice in my head asked me to think about my wife and children. It said, "This is not a good time." I found the strength to sit up and grab my phone to call the emergency services. I saw a man smiling at me and nodding in the corner of the room and then I blacked out.

The next thing I knew I was waking up in a French

hospital after having a heart operation. My wife had flown over with our two children and they were all sitting round my bed. My wife told me that I had died twice on the way to the hospital.

The strangest thing is that whilst I was hearing voices telling me to look after my health, my wife was hearing voices telling her that I was in danger. We believe it could only be the angels who were looking out for us that day.

Life-changing Moments

As well as at times of immediate danger, angels often seem to make themselves known to us when we are at one of life's many turning points. Our choices at these moments can define the directions our life takes in the future, and we are often in spiritual crisis at times when we are forced to choose between two paths. It makes sense that angels might understand our emotional turmoil at such time, and perhaps choose those precise moments to give us a helping hand.

Tom, 38

The worst day of my life, without doubt, was the day I found out my wife had been having an affair with one of her colleagues. I had found suspicious texts from him on her phone, and while I had no reason to suspect anything, I confronted her with what I had found.

I think I expected her to tell me it was all a misunderstanding, but instead she just started crying and admitted that she had had a fling with him. She assured me it was all over and kept saying sorry, but I just couldn't accept what had happened.

That night I slept in the spare room and I left the house at dawn the next day before she could wake up. I was furious at her, and I also felt humiliated. I wasn't really thinking straight and all I could think about was revenge. I wanted to go and punch the man but I didn't know his address.

I went to work, but I couldn't concentrate. As soon as I could sneak away I drove into the nearest town and booked myself into a hotel, without letting my wife know where I was. Then I went out and started drinking. I just wanted to forget everything.

When the pub closed I went to a club. I wasn't bothered about dancing, but I wanted to get drunk and I didn't feel like being on my own. I started talking to a girl at the bar. One thing led to another and I invited her back to my hotel. She knew I was married but I guess she had had a few drinks to and she didn't seem concerned about it. At the time this seemed like a kind of revenge on my wife.

In the hotel, she went to the bathroom and I sat waiting for her on the bed. She took a long time, but I didn't think anything of it. But when she came out she had a really strange look on her face.

She told me that she had seen an angel, and that she had to go. To start with I thought it was a joke, but she was completely serious. She told me that what we were doing was wrong and she couldn't stay. I was disappointed, to say the least, but I didn't try to persuade her to stay. To be honest I just wondered if she was some kind of religious nut.

I slept for a while but woke with a headache very early the next day, just as the sun was coming up. I went for a walk through the town and felt sick when I thought about how close I had come to doing something stupid the night before. But still I was angry at my wife and didn't know what to do.

Everything in the town seemed very clean and nice at that time of day. There was a park there and I lay down on my back and closed my eyes. I tried to clear my mind of all the bad things that were circling through it. And then for the first time ever I felt the presence of an angel myself. The angel didn't exactly appear to me, but I had a very strong sense of being in the presence of something wonderful. Perhaps this was the same angel that the girl had seen the night before. And I felt that the angel was telling me that instead of thinking about myself I needed to ask myself why this had happened. I needed to think about my wife and how she must be feeling.

I started to remember all the times she had been unhappy and I hadn't understood. All the times I had been selfish, all the times we hadn't talked about the important things we needed to talk about. The anger in me didn't magically go away, but I started to see a more complicated picture. Rather than just think about how she had betrayed me, I started to wonder why.

I'm not going to pretend that the rest of the story was easy. I knew I had to go home and talk to her properly and that is exactly what I did. I even had to apologise for running away instead of talking to her. I hated doing that but as soon as I did, she started crying and told me how worried she had been. I could see that at the very least she did still care about me.

It was a painful conversation and things were very difficult for a while. But that moment in the park was the moment when I realised I had to fight for my marriage and to do this with my wife, instead of just seeing it from my own point of view. In a way I see it as one of the moments in my life when I grew up and became a bit less childish.

Today our marriage is stronger than ever. But I could so easily have taken a different turn that day, and I grateful that something steered me back in the right direction.

Chloe, 33

It changes your life when you have a child. So imagine how my life changed when my first pregnancy turned out to be triplets.

I had absolutely no idea how we were going to cope. When they let me and my husband take the triplets home, he was excited but I was petrified. I had to learn all about feeding them, bathing them, getting them to sleep and all that, but three times over. At the hospital the nurses had helped, but it was just the five of us.

Of course, my family and friends promised to help as much as they could (and they were wonderful). But still I was very worried.

That night, we finally managed to get them all to sleep at once. I was about ready to pass out on my feet from exhaustion. I sat down and had a cup of tea. Then I went into the nursery for one last look at them before I went to lie down myself.

The three of them were lying there looking perfectly beautiful and calm. And behind them I saw a very distinct human shape, made of light. I could just make out the angel's face, and she was looking down at the babies. As I stared at her, she looked up at me just for a moment and then I blinked and couldn't see her any more.

I knew that I had a heavy responsibility looking after these children. But it was wonderfully calming to know that I wasn't going to have to do it all on my own.

Anya, 51

I have suffered from depression for many years. It is hard to say why it comes and goes, but when I am at my worst I find it extremely difficult to get out of that slump of hopelessness. It feels like there is no point even trying, because I can't imagine anything that would make me happy.

One of the low points of my depression came in my thirties. In many ways it was inexplicable. I was married to a man I loved, and I had two young children who were wonderful. But I just felt these waves of depression coming over me every day and it got worse and worse.

Then it started to affect my family. It was difficult for my husband because he tried as hard as he could to help me out, but I just got annoyed at his attempts to "cheer me up". Even worse, it started to affect my children. They would find me crying in the kitchen and ask me why and while I tried to keep myself together for them, I knew I was making them sad, too.

I reached the point where I couldn't bear to let anyone touch me or come near me, and every night I spent in the spare room, crying or staring at the ceiling. And in the day I was like a zombie. I managed to do the bare minimum to look after the children, but really I felt like a worthless mother.

One day I told my husband I needed some time away. He could have reacted by being angry or by refusing to make arrangements to help me out. Instead, he just agreed that I did need some time to myself and that was, perhaps, more frightening. It proved that things really were bad. And also I was scared that he was getting ready to split up with me, and that I would lose everything.

He arranged for temporary childcare and I rented a room in a small town by the lake. I also saw a doctor and got some medication that helped me sleep. Medication is never the long term solution to depression, but sometimes it can help you to get back on an even keel.

So there I was in this small town all by myself with nothing to do but think and try to get my head straight. For the first week I didn't do much except sleep and stare at the television in my room. I was still feeling terrible and couldn't motivate myself to go outside except when I ran out of essentials. I was barely eating and was losing weight.

After a week I woke up one day and felt like I could go outside. I went for a walk out by the lake. But then another wave of the hopeless feeling came over me and I started crying, looking out at the lake.

At this point a woman came up to me and asked me why I was crying. I couldn't even talk I felt so bad. Then she did a wonderful thing. She simply walked up to me and gave me a big hug and told me everything would be alright. Remember that this was at a time when I was scared of being touched, but for some reason I just let her do it, and this wonderful warm feeling went right through my body.

We stood there like that and I managed to stop crying. Then, when I was ready, we sat down and talked. I told her all sorts of things about my childhood and my early relationships. Things I had never told anyone, not even a therapist. And she just listened while I poured out all these things. She was wonderful to talk to, and I felt like I was understanding some of the reasons why I get depressed for the first time,

Then she walked back with me to the apartment and told me I needed to sleep. And that was that. I never saw her again. But when I woke in the morning, I felt for the first time in months like I wanted to be alive.

I got up and ate a huge breakfast and drove straight back to my family. I was worried when I saw my husband but I knew that the first thing I wanted to do was to give him a hug like the one she had given me. Before he even had a chance to talk I had my arms around him and he just held me, too. Then my children came out and hugged my legs so it turned into this funny kind of family hug.

I can't honestly say if that woman was an angel or not. I don't remember much about how she looked, only the warm feeling I had when I was with her. I never went back to that town to try and find her again. I do know that she changed my life.

The biggest single thing she did for me was to teach me that sometimes when I was at my most bleak I wanted to push people away. But what I actually need at those moments is the exact opposite. I need to be close to the people I love. I want to push them away because I am scared of hurting them or disappointing them, so I feel that distance is the only solution. But it is the complete opposite – it makes things worse and then I get into a spiral where I hurt them and push them further away.

I talked about all these things with my husband that night and it was a big turning point. Whoever the woman was, she really helped me. I still get depressed but from that time onwards I have never got as bad as I used to get because I have finally started to learn how to deal with it.

Alan, 46

I used to work as a manager in a bar. I was going through a strange time in my life and I took to staying after hours on my own, listening to music on the jukebox and drinking a few beers before I went home. This was on top of having had a few drinks through the evening, and soon without realising, I was starting to become something of an alcoholic.

I started to finish the evening with a few whiskeys. Several times I fell asleep there, slumped over a table on my own, and woke up with a start some time in the small hours. Once I was asleep for so long I only just managed to get everything cleaned up and locked up in time for the guy who ran the bar at lunchtimes to show up. I literally ran into him walking down the street just after I left and had to make up a story about how I had stayed over at a friend's house (since he knew I didn't live in that neighbourhood.)

I knew I was drifting into trouble but I felt unable to do anything about it. Until, one night when I drifted off to sleep there once again and was woken by what felt like feathers tickling my face. I woke up and there was an angel sitting across the table from me, a man in white clothes with light around his arms.

He smiled at me, but he looked serious. He told me that enough was enough and that I needed to sort myself out. I told him he was right, and then he just stood up and walked out the door. As soon as he was gone I went and checked the door and it was locked with the shutters down, but when he went through it he opened it perfectly easily and walked out into a bright light.

I responded to this immediately. I went home and got myself washed up and shaved. Then I went in the next day to my boss and told him I was quitting. I had no idea what I was going to do. I just knew that I needed to get myself away from that environment where it was too easy for me to just indulge myself.

I had to work my notice out but I was careful not to drink through those days, and he found someone to replace me just a week later. The same day I went and got a job helping to shift office furniture from a depot downtown. It was hard physical labour and exhausting, but the guys I was working with were great fun.

As soon as I left that job my life started to improve. I think it was basically a moment when I could either slump further into self-pity and trouble or I could get a grip. By getting a grip I took the first step to making my life better.

I didn't completely stop drinking. I don't think I am actually an alcoholic, I just need to stay out of an environment that puts too many temptations in my way.

These days I enjoy a drink after work but I know when to stop.

I really should have been able to make those changes myself without intervention, but my will power was weak at that moment and seeing that angel was just what I needed to make me take a step back and see myself through someone else's eyes.

Dan, 35

When I was fifteen I began to realise that I was gay and decided to come out to my family. Their reaction really upset me. They were very angry, telling me that it was just a phase that I was going through and that I'd grow out of it. I spent three miserable days in my room feeling as if my world had ended.

Eventually, I went downstairs and took my father's whisky bottle up to my room and got some painkillers from the bathroom. I went in my room determined to take them all. I had a sip of whisky and took the pills. I remember feeling woozy and then drifting off to sleep. I was woken by a soft voice saying, "Don't do this".

When I opened my eyes there was a beautiful woman sitting on my bed holding my hand. She said that things would get better with my family and they didn't want to lose me. The next thing I knew I woke up in a hospital bed. Something had made my mum come up to my room and when she saw what I'd done she called an ambulance. They pumped my stomach and I pulled through.

My parents were so upset that I'd resorted to suicide and told me that they would accept me however I wanted to live my life. That was fifteen years ago and I'm now living with my boyfriend and my family are completely OK with it. We often have them round for Sunday dinner. I know that the angel I saw that day saved my life

Jake, 47

I was an alcoholic. Originally I was just a social drinker, then I started to drink more or less every day, and gradually it started to affect my life. My marriage fell apart, I lost a good job and had to get a telesales job I hated just to survive. I lost a lot of good friends in that period also.

I never accepted that I was an alcoholic. So far as I was concerned the fact that I didn't drink in the daytime, and could occasionally take a day without a drink meant that I wasn't dependent. Even though I would often go to the pub straight from work, then buy a pack of beer to drink at home until I passed out from drink, I saw it as something I just did to relieve the boredom and stress of life.

Then I met a new woman and started going out with her regularly. For a while I cut down on the drinking and things were looking up. However, the old habits started to creep back. Even though I could see I was starting to drive her away, I would arrive for dates having already had a few drinks, and started to call her late at night rambling about my ex-wife when I had had too much to drink.

No surprise that she decided to finish with me after a few weeks of that behaviour. And then I used that blow as an excuse to start drinking even more. Now I was drinking spirits, vodka or tequila, on a daily basis, and again it was starting to cause trouble at work as I was often late or simply didn't show up.

One Monday I woke up after a heavy session feeling terrible and remorseful, and I realised that someone was sitting on the end of my bed. It was a man, who talked to me about all the things I was doing to myself.

He told me that it was my choice what I did, and that I didn't need excuses to do the right thing or to do the wrong thing. He told me that my drinking was destroying me and that this was my choice, too. And then he just got up and walked out of the apartment.

It was eerie. I knew that everything he had said was true, and that only someone who knew me well could know so much about the little lies you tell yourself to justify the next drink, the next session.

I even used to be pleased if something bad happened because it gave me an excuse to get drunk. And then eventually I just didn't care because every day I knew would end up drinking myself into oblivion.

I sat up in bed and thought hard about my life. I made some immediate decisions. For the first time I realised I was actually an alcoholic. I really didn't think I could fix it on my own, so I decided to give everything up. I gave notice on my apartment, quit my job and went home to my parents' house. I had to beg forgiveness for some bad things I had done, but once they realised I was owning up to being an alcoholic they welcomed me. They had been pretty angry about some of the mistakes I had made but they were prepared to help me so long as I was prepared to help myself.

I only stayed there for a couple of months, and for once I parted from my family on good terms. I just needed the time out to get the alcohol out of my system for good. Then I moved to a new city and made a fresh start, this time without the crutch of alcohol to get me through hard times. I went to AA meetings. I didn't do the whole 12 step thing, but I really appreciated the support of other people who understood the things I had been through.

I won't pretend it was easy. So many times I wanted a drink, but the one thing that always got me through was remembering what I had been told by the angel, if that's what he was. He had told me that it was my choice what I did. And now, when something bad happened, instead of using it as an excuse to drink, I sat down and thought about what I really needed to do. I knew that turning to drink was an option I had but that it was my choice only if I did that and that I couldn't blame life, or other people, or my job. I ended up going to the gym a lot – I decided that if I had a tendency to addictive behaviour, it was far better to be addicted to exercise than to drinking and I got much fitter as a result.

Life is much better for me now. I know I have to live it on my own and that I have to make my own choices. Some of them work out, some of them don't but I am proud that I managed to get beyond that dependency on alcohol, and grateful for the help I had getting from there to here.

Hilary, 32

I suffered from dreadful shyness when I was young. I was fine with my mother and father, but as soon as I had to deal with anyone else, I would just curl up in embarrassment and be unable to talk properly. I had a slight stutter and I had moved around a lot of different schools and when I hit the start of the teenage years I just disappeared into myself.

My mother knew I was going through a difficult time and tried to help me but I just closed myself off from her so that she couldn't help me. I had no friends, and I could go for weeks without having a proper conversation with anyone. I was also starting to harm myself in small ways, and I wasn't in good shape physically because I spent so long hiding away in dark places.

It sounds weird but the turning point came just before I left home. I was going to go away to college and I was absolutely dreading it. My time in high school had been pretty awful, although the bright side was that I had done well academically. Mainly because I spent so much time on my own with my books.

One night I had an extremely vivid dream. An angel came and talked to me about how I felt about going away. She had a kind of silvery glow around her, and she was obviously a spirit. She told me to remember two things. First, she told me to talk to my mother. And I solemnly promised I would do that.

Secondly she told me no-one was stopping me from making friends except myself. I couldn't pretend it was other people's fault, when I wouldn't even give them the chance. Then she left me there.

In the morning I was curled up in anxiety because I had made that promise. I wanted to pretend it hadn't happened because then I could have gone on as though everything was fine, but it was such a vivid memory and I knew things couldn't get much worse.

So I sat my mother down and talked to her about everything I felt. Two things surprised me. Firstly she wasn't angry at me for not fitting in, and "being normal". If anything she was relieved that I had finally owned up to the problems – obviously she knew I was in trouble but hadn't known how to get through to me.

The other thing was that she confessed that she had harmed herself as a teenager. In her case it had been a case of depression and teen angst rather than shyness, but I was astonished when she told me this. My confident mother who always seemed so in charge and in control had been just as mixed up and confused as me when she was younger. She even showed me some scars on her upper arms – I had seen them before but she had told me some story about being scratched badly by a cat, but it turns out they came from one time she cut herself when she was sixteen.

I think that's the thing that really shook me into looking at myself differently. If she could change, then surely I could. I had been thinking that there was something especially wrong with me, but actually I was pretty normal. And I had plenty of opportunity to improve my life.

So I went to college with, at the very least, the determination to move on and the understanding that it was possible. I didn't turn into an extrovert overnight, of course. But I forced myself to go outside my comfort zone.

The first night I was there I introduced myself to the girl in the next room and she invited me in for coffee. And, of course, it turned out she was pretty nervous at being away from home, too, so we at least had that in common. She ended up being a good friend.

I also made myself go and join some clubs and to talk to people I might never have considered speaking to before. I still stuttered sometimes, but I found that if I talked to people about it they didn't treat me badly because of it. Not everyone is as mean as high school kids. And slowly, I turned things round and overcame the worst of the shyness.

The reason I think the person I talked to in the dream really was an angel was that they knew that my mother was the right person for me to talk to. It seemed like they knew that she had been through some of the same things as me and that she was the person who could help to sort my head out at that stage of my life.

Darren, 34

About ten years ago I was on a train going home after visiting one of my friends. I had been in a dark place at the time and decided as I travelled home that I would end my life. I just couldn't see a future for myself.

We stopped in a station and a young man, probably in his early twenties, got on the train and asked me if he could sit down. I said yes but I was secretly irritated because there were other vacant seats and I felt so depressed that I wanted to sit alone. I decided to fake sleep to get out of any conversation.

I felt myself gradually drifting off to sleep and then felt the young man place his jacket over me which I thought strange but for some reason I didn't mind.

I think I must have been asleep the rest of the journey home. I remember waking up at my station and the young man got off the train with me. He smiled at me and I felt so calm and peaceful, I even began to feel a glimmer of hope that things would eventually get better. He had lovely deep blue eyes and when I turned to say goodbye to him he just stood beside me smiling.

As I walked out of the station there was no one around except the young man and myself. At the top of the station road I turned to see which way he was walking but I couldn't see anyone. There is only one road leading in and out of our station and everyone leaving the station has to use it. I couldn't think where he would have gone to.

When I got home that night, I no longer felt suicidal and could even say that I could start to look forward to the future. I think the young man was my guardian angel come to save my life.

Iain, 62

On my fiftieth birthday I was in Turkey. I had recently gone through a rather painful divorce and I was on holiday trying to get over it. I was in a bad place emotionally.

I got up in the morning and it was such a beautiful day I decided to go for a walk. I took my rucksack with some water and bread and cheese and set off up the nearest mountain. I call it a mountain, really it is just a rocky hill, but it is a long way up and a fairly gruelling walk. It took me about three hours on the way up. I didn't see anyone on the way up.

I stopped close to the peak to enjoy the view and for a well earned drink and snack. At that point a man walked down from the peak, out of the bright sun which was above the rocks. When he reached me he stopped and said hello in English. I offered him some water as he didn't seem to have any, and he sat down next to me.

We started to chat, and for some reason I started to tell him all about myself. He was a very good listener and had the kind of face you instinctively trust. I had been bottling up a lot of feelings about my wife – I was sad we had fallen out of love and felt devastated that I was separated from my two daughters. I saw them at weekends but it just isn't the same thing as being there with them every day.

So I told him all about it, and he just sat and listened, watching me with those kind eyes. Then he talked to me about some couples he had known who had split up and told me their stories. He told me that I was in the most difficult phase but that things would get better over time, that if I didn't turn my wife into a bad person in my mind I would remember why I had loved her in the first place.

He also told me that my daughters would be missing me and that I had every chance of seeing a great deal of them and playing an important role in their lives when they were older and had left home.

Above all he kept reminding me that I loved these people and that as long as I made sure they knew that, things would work out for the best in the end. This was an important thing for me to hear. I think I had been backing myself into a corner – thinking that I couldn't hold on to my family so I had to push them away and leave them to get on with their lives. But that wasn't what I wanted at all.

We talked for a good half an hour up there, and he told me so many things about myself that I started to feel as if he had known me a long time. That's why I think of him as being an angel – it seems too much of a coincidence that he simply turned up in my hour of need and was so wise and helpful.

Then finally he shook my hand and set off down the slope. I sat for about ten minutes thinking about what he had told me, then set off after him in the same direction. I wondered if I might catch him up as he was older than me. But I didn't see him again. The path weaved down the mountain but there were many parts where I could see large sections of it below me and I didn't see him once.

When I got home I wrote long letters to my wife and to each of my daughters. They were very emotional letters, and difficult to write. I am naturally reticent and find it hard to open up to people. To my wife I wrote a letter thanking her for our years of marriage and apologising for the things I had got wrong, but saying how much I hoped we would stay friends. To each of my daughters I wrote letters telling them how much I loved them and looked forward to seeing them getting older and turning into grown women.

It was a cathartic day. On one level I was finally adjusting to the idea that the marriage really was over and I wanted my wife to know I had come to understand that. But at the same time that man made me understand that I could move on in life and could retain some of the love and friendship I had once had in my family.

Today my ex-wife and I both have new partners in our lives. She remarried five years ago, while I have been going out with my partner for a similar amount of time. I am happy to say that we have managed to stay friends. The letters I wrote that day meant a lot to her and my daughters – they all contacted me in their own ways over the following weeks and we had some difficult but valuable conversations. I don't see my ex-wife every week or even every month, but we do talk and share memories without the bitterness I used to feel.

Three weeks ago I gave my youngest daughter away at her marriage. My ex-wife was there and both our partners came. It was a beautiful, happy occasion and one of the proudest moments of my life. There was a strange moment just after the bride and groom exchanged vows where I had a sudden, very clear memory of the face of that man I met on the mountain. Once again he was smiling and I came close to crying thinking back on how far I had come since that day.

Juliet, 25

Towards the end of my time at college I became very depressed. I had trouble bothering to do anything and even though I had always done well in my studies, I just didn't see the point.

Everything depended on my final exams. I needed to pass them to graduate from the college. But on the first morning of the exams I was lying there in bed and suddenly I just couldn't see the point in going. I was at that stage where everything seems pointless and the idea that my going to the exam would make any difference to anything important seemed laughable.

I decided not to bother and turned over to go to sleep. But as soon as I closed my eyes I saw this face. It was a loving face but a very stern one. I could see it was disappointed in me. And the words came into my head – it might not matter if you fail, but in that case it won't matter if you try either.

That had never occurred to me. It was a bit of a revelation, I could just go to the exam, see what happened and it still wouldn't make any difference. So that's what I did, I just went and did what I could, and did the same for all the other exams. I still had that feeling it was pointless, but that moment had persuaded me that not doing it was just as pointless.

Obviously, in retrospect, this was still a bit of a depressed attitude, but it's what got me through the exams, and that was all that was needed at that moment.

I passed. Not spectacularly, but I did OK. Then I went away for the summer and fell in love and then fell out of love and went home, and then wondered what to do next. At this stage I wasn't depressed any more. The idea I had seriously considered throwing three years of education away seemed laughable and I was grateful I'd had my mind changed.

Eventually I got a job. And it was a job I loved, one that I'd never have got if I'd just given in to the depression. My life has moved on from there and has turned out to be interesting and worthwhile.

This can't be useful advice in all situations with depressives. But sometimes all a depressed person needs is someone to give them a bit of a push in the right direction to stop them making a foolish decision that will wreck their lives. I didn't have anyone there to do that for me, but instead I had some kind of angel help me out and make sure I didn't behave like a complete idiot.

Calvin, 32

I've always had a short temper and used to get into a lot of fights. My stepfather would hit me as a kid and I guess I learned from him to use violence to solve problems.

I think it was an angel that turned my life around. I was in a local bar, which is known for being rough. I'd had a few drinks and was playing pool. My girlfriend of the time was talking to a man at the bar, which was enough to make me start to lose my temper. Then later in the evening, he walked past me and accidentally pushed my elbow.

I didn't actually spill my drink, but it was a close thing, and I shouted something at him. He just gave me this annoying "chill out" gesture.

This the typical kind of moment when something in me would snap. I watched him walk away, feeling the red mist come over me. I grabbed a pool cue and took a few steps in his direction.

Then someone took my arm. It was a man, older than me, looking quite distinguished. I'm absolutely sure he hadn't been there in the bar before. He just whispered in my ear, "Think about it…" And there was this flash of images in my mind. I saw myself attacking the guy who had barged me, and him lying on the ground with blood coming from his head. I saw a woman crying. I saw the police taking me away and putting me in a jail cell. It takes longer to say what I saw than it did for it to flash through my mind.

I turned to look at the man, to ask who he was but he just gave me a serious look and walked away. It was very strange. When I had lost my temper before, I had never thought about possible consequences. It just seemed like he knew this was a moment when something really bad was likely to happen and chose to let me know about it, to give me the choice of making a different choice.

I just put the pool cue down, and walked out of the bar, without telling anyone. I went home and thought about all the fights I had been in and wondered why it had seemed so important to me to prove I could beat someone in a fight.

Next day I went to church. It wasn't to pray, I just wanted someone to talk to. I talked to the minister there and he was very helpful and understanding. He suggested some support groups I could go to, but also told me that if I was asking myself these questions I was already heading in the right direction.

These days I do go to church once a week. I don't really know what I believe in but I find it is a good place to feel calm and to remember the progress I have made in life. I have more or less given up drinking, and haven't had a fight since that time in the bar. In general my life is much better. It's a lot easier to hang on to a job if you aren't always turning up with black eyes and cuts on your face, for a start.

I'm just glad I never seriously injured anyone or, God forbid, killed them. It could easily have happened and I do believe that might have been what happened that night if the angel hadn't intervened.

Ruth, 47

During the credit crunch, my family lost a great deal of money. We had this accountant who had invested our money for us and a lot of it simply disappeared as it was invested in bad schemes and banks that went under. There is a group of us still trying to get some money back as it seems the accountant was using some dubious practises, but honestly I don't think we will see any of it again.

The day my husband found out, he realised he had to come home and tell me that we would have to sell our house. He'd already taken a cut in salary and now we had no savings or investments to speak of. He knew that it was going to upset me. In fact I think he thought I would be angry and blame him for everything. Effectively we were in a position of having to start over having saved up all that money over the years and he was stunned and terrified.

He drove part of the way home and then stopped for a coffee, a couple of miles away from our house. He told me he was basically frozen with fear, anger, and confusion. At this point he seriously considered killing himself. He suddenly decided that the best thing for everyone would be if he had an accident on the way home. He has life insurance so this would perhaps have meant I would have got a pay-out and been able to keep the house.

He knew how much I loved that house. I wanted it as soon as I saw it and had put my heart and soul into making it nice to live in. We had been there for the last ten years that my daughters were living at home and now their rooms were always there for them when they came to visit.

So, he went out to the car, determined to end everything. He'd decided to head for the freeway and drive off the road on a stretch where he would have a long fall. He actually felt quite happy about his decision and was thinking it was the right thing to do.

When he got into the car, he found the ignition wouldn't work. It was refusing to recognise the key. They have these security devices on them and this does sometimes happen, but usually you can get it to work by relocking and unlocking the car. This time, he simply couldn't get it to work, no matter what he tried. He got out of the car and walked around it, trying the remote key device in different positions, without luck.

At that stage an old guy walked up to him. My husband tells me he looked a bit like Clarence the angel in *It's a Wonderful Life* but he might be giving himself a bit of poetic license on retelling the story. Anyway, it was an old guy with white hair who asked my dad what he was doing.

When he explained, the guy told him it would probably be best to leave it till the morning. He said that everything seems to get better in the morning, then walked off leaving my husband feeling a bit foolish.

He ended up leaving the car there and walking home. By the time he got home his crazy idea about killing himself had started to seem like a stupid whim.

He told me all about the money. And I did cry and I believe I did shout a bit. He wasn't wrong to expect that, I am quite volatile. But then we ended up realising that crying and shouting wasn't going to help anyone and started making proper plans.

It was late that night in bed he apologetically told me about how he had considered killing himself. I told him that if he had done that I'd never have spoken to him again. Which made us laugh, because it was such a silly response. But I was furious he had considered it and relieved he hadn't managed to go through with it. As he said, the old man seemed like an angel who simply wouldn't let him do it.

So we simply got on with working out how we would cope without our savings. I won't pretend it has been easy. We didn't manage to hang on to the house, and even where we live now we have had to take in lodgers. I have had to go back to work and we are gradually starting to build up a nest egg again. We will never get back to where we were before the recession. But actually in some ways it has brought us closer together again as we have had to work as a team and look at things in a new light.

I don't think he'll ever consider killing himself again. But if he does I hope there is another angel there to make sure his car won't start.

Linda, 38

I ran away from my husband and two children a few years ago. I had been unhappy for a while, stuck at home looking after the kids. I loved them but I was so unhappy I started to convince myself they'd be better off without me.

I thought if I just ran away and left them then my husband would be free to find someone else who would be better for him, better for the kids. I think I was rationalising my feelings of claustrophobia and panic about getting older.

One day when the children were at nursery I went home, packed a bag and left a note for my husband asking him to look after the kids and forget about me. I took my little car and drove a hundred miles to this little town I'd once visited. I didn't have a lot of money but I knew I'd need a few days in a bed and breakfast before I could find work and a place to stay.

I stayed there that night and barely slept. It was a weird mixture of excitement, fear and guilt. I felt that having run away like that I had made an irreversible decision and that I could never go back. That scared me but also I wanted to get on with my life and try to live completely differently.

Next day, I bought a sandwich and took it to a little park. I sat on a bench feeding the ducks the last bit of my bread. Then I realised there was a man sitting on the bench next to me. He was quite old, with white hair and a very kind face.

He asked how I was and for some strange reason I told him the whole story. He seemed so trustworthy and while I had been planning this I had had to keep everything a big secret.

He listened to me and asked about my plans. He didn't judge me or tell me I was making a mistake. He just patiently asked me about the reasons why I felt I had to run away and what my expectations and hopes for the future were.

To start with I was feeling like I had made a great decision and I was kind of boasting to him about it. Then as I kept talking and as he kept asking questions, I felt more and more of an idiot. I saw myself through his eyes and realised how selfish I was being. Then I suddenly had a clear image of my kids and thought about how I'd never see them growing up and I felt desolate.

In the end he said only one thing I clearly remember. He told me that wherever I went I couldn't run away from myself. And he also told me that it was never too late to change a decision.

Then he shook my hand and looked into my eyes. That was the moment when I felt I was talking to an angel. It was something I saw in his eyes, something ancient and wise, and when he touched me I felt a kind of shock as though I was suddenly seeing everything covered in the brightest light imaginable.

Then he just walked off and left me there.

I went back to my room and sat staring at the wall for about an hour turning everything over and over in my mind. I still knew I could keep going and not look back. I could leave them behind and try to make a new life. But like he had said, I would still be the same person underneath and the regrets would always be there.

It was the most difficult thing I have ever done, but I packed my bag, paid up and headed home. I was shaking with fear because I still thought it might be too late, that my husband might be so angry he wouldn't let me come back.

It took me five minutes to get out of the car when I parked at our house, I was so scared. Then I went in and found my husband crawling on the floor playing with my son with a toy lorry.

He was furious as I'd thought, asking me what the hell I'd been playing at. But also he came and grabbed me and told me how terrified he'd been and how much he loved me. That meant a lot to me. I'd been feeling very unloved and abandoned. So even though he was angry I realised he did still need me.

I can't pretend everything magically got better overnight. But it was a turning point. Our marriage had come that close to falling apart, we both realised we had to work much harder at it and to be honest with each other about the problems.

Every day I am with my kids I give thanks that I didn't go through with it. They are the loves of my life and they have a brilliant father. I would have been a fool to throw it away. So, even though it was a terribly difficult thing to do, to come back and face up to what I had nearly done, it was the best decision I ever made. With a little bit of help along the way.

Everyday Angels

Happily, it is not only in times of great emotional crisis or danger that angels appear to us. In the accounts in this section we see angels manifesting themselves in the most ordinary of circumstances: as a mother hangs out the washing, as a man takes his daily run, and as children sleep.

These accounts have a special charm as they show us people living ordinary lives, but being made aware of the interconnection between the spiritual and material realms.

Sally, 25

I saw an angel standing by my aunt's grave once.

I was visiting to take her some flowers and as I walked towards the grave I saw a tall graceful figure standing looking down at the gravestone. I was surprised to see anyone else there. It is usually only me and my mother who visit the grave, and my mother was at work.

I wanted to find out who this person was, so I hurried on. I had to walk round a holly bush and when I came out the other side the figure was gone. It was impossible that someone could have walked away without coming down the path past me as the grave is in a corner of the church yard.

I am certain it was an angel I saw that day. My aunt was a beautiful person who meant a great deal to me. It makes me happy to think that an angel cared about her, too.

Luisa, 42

The first time I saw an angel, I was hanging some clothes out in the garden. I was thinking what a beautiful day it was. It was an early autumn day with a sharp breeze, a blue sky with a few clouds scudding across it and the leaves on the trees were starting to turn.

And then from the corner of my eye I saw the angel at the end of the garden. It was a figure the size of a person, but there was a kind of light around it (I wasn't sure if it was a "him" or a "her"). I didn't turn and stare straight at the angel, I just glanced in that direction. The angel seemed to be smiling and was aware of me looking at it. Then the next time I looked it was gone.

I felt lucky to have a glimpse of the angel. It made me feel that they are always there watching over us but we aren't always lucky enough to see them.

I have had similar experiences a few times since then. Once in the supermarket I saw a young mother walking her child in a stroller and behind her I could see the presence of an angel, a figure made of light clearly following her. Once I drove past an automobile accident. It looked quite bad, and the emergency services were trying to cut someone out of the car. Beside the car there were two angels clearly visible, looking on with worry and concern.

I don't know why I have been lucky enough to have these experiences. There is nothing special about me and I have never had any terrible experiences where an angel had to help me. I guess I am just fortunate, or blessed.

Peter, 37

I have never seen an angel. But when my son Thomas first started to talk he often used to talk about an angel that he saw.

To start with he would just mention "the lady" he had seen. He would tell me that the lady had been in his room watching him when he woke up. Or if he fell and hurt himself he would say that the lady had given him a hug.

To start with I didn't pay much attention as it seemed like one of those funny things children say. They often have imaginary friends, don't they?

One day in church the reading mentioned angels and Thomas asked me about them, and I told him what I could. He told me that the lady he saw was an angel.

I didn't believe him at first. But the more he told me about her, the more convinced I was. He described her as being a lady of about my age wearing beautiful clothes. He said there was always a light behind her when he saw her and she always came when he needed her, like when he was feeling sad or lonely.

If he had told me all these things after he heard about angels in the church I might have thought he was making it up. But he had been talking about the lady since he was about three years old and it was only when he was five years old that he made the connection between the lady and the angels he heard about.

Over time he mentioned her less often. I wonder if small children can see angels more easily because they are so innocent and because they don't have any preconceptions about the things they experience?

He is ten now and hasn't talked about the angel for a few years. But I really hope she is still looking after him, even if he doesn't see her any more.

Marilyn, 29

One autumn I was taking my little girl, who was four at the time, for a walk, and feeling very sad because my mum had been told that she had breast cancer. Suddenly I felt something touch my arm and I turned round to see a woman standing there.

She told me that everything was going to be OK and then handed me a little bunch of flowers. I showed the little posy to my daughter who was delighted with it. I turned round to thank the woman but she had gone, there was no one there.

About six months later, my mother, who had responded well to treatment, was told that her cancer was in remission. To celebrate we decided to go to the local cats' home and get her a cat. She had lost her last cat shortly before she became ill and hadn't wanted to get another in case her cancer couldn't be cured.

The cat she fell in love with was a large stripy ginger cat who also took to her immediately and rubbed around her legs purring. We told the staff that she was the one and asked what she was called. The answer was, "Flower".

Alison, 33

I see an angel on the sea sometimes. Where I live, we have to take a boat to get across to the mainland shops. (There is a long way round by road but it is much more convenient to take the boat trip.)

I have a great respect for the sea, I am very experienced in the water and usually know exactly how safe it is to travel. If a storm blows up, I simply don't get into the boat and I find a different solution instead . However, there was one time when I was in a hurry and decided to risk the crossing in choppy weather. The storm got worse as I got out into the middle and the waves were getting quite alarming. It was nothing like a near death experience. I had a lifejacket, so even if I had lost control or capsized I would almost certainly have been fine.

However, it was pretty scary at the time and I was really struggling with the waves. I had to gather up the loose paraphernalia on the deck and stow it in the cabin as it looked to be in danger of getting swept over, but by the time I had done that there was a lot of water on deck and the waves were getting fiercer.

That was the first time I saw the angel. He was at the prow of the boat, looking towards the lights of our cottage across the bay. He looked back at me for a moment and then back towards the shore. His gaze was very calm but I sensed that he was there for me if I needed him.

I was too busy to think too hard about it. I had to tend to the engine and keep adjusting the direction to make sure we cut through the waves and didn't get pushed too far out. When I finally got back to the jetty, I couldn't see the angel any more. My brother was waiting for me. I was really relieved because it was so rough by now that I was going to have a hard time tying up, but he helped me and I got safely on to shore.

He was furious at me for taking the risk on crossing. He had heard what sounded like a knock at the door. Afterwards he thought the knock was the wind, but I suspected that might have been connected to the angel also.

My life probably wasn't in danger, but on the other hand it was one of the stupider things I have done and I have learned a lesson from it. You can never be too careful.

Since then I have seen the same angel two more times. Not in stormy weather, just on ordinary calm days when I have suddenly noticed him there at the prow of the boat. He is not always easy to see, it can look like he is there one moment and then gone the next but I am convinced I do see him. I am not so egotistical to assume he is there especially for me. If anything I tend to imagine he is a spirit of the water who looks after people who go out to sea in that area.

A long time ago they used to have angels as figureheads on boats and ships. I always assumed it was simply a religious superstition, but now it occurs to me to wonder if sailors of the past saw angels at the front of their boats and did them homage by carving their likeness in wood. When I think about the sailors of the past I always think about how dangerous their lives must have been out on the ocean. Even today the life of a fisherman is a very dangerous one. No wonder that people see angels out at sea, when we can so suddenly find ourselves at death's door out there.

Mel, 21

When I was fifteen I was such a mess. I suffered from terrible anxiety attacks which led to depression with suicidal feelings. Getting on the school bus was a nightmare. I would feel so nervous that it made me feel sick. If anyone so much as looked at me I would feel my face turn bright red and my heart rate start to pound.

One day I started to pray, "Please help me, God," over and over again, silently. I was sitting on my own on the bus as usual but suddenly I began to feel this warm friendly feeling beside me. It was as if I was being wrapped in warm, comforting blankets. It really made me feel happier. For once, when I got off the bus at school I wasn't dreading the day ahead.

That day, when I arrived in homeroom, there was a new girl. Like me, she wore glasses; like me, she didn't have a figure you'd want to show off, but I felt that she was a really important girl.

She was someone that you were just drawn to, and wanted to be friends with. She had what I'd always seen as my 'problems' but she was cool. Because I was sitting on my own she was directed to sit next to me.

At first, I was scared that she would spend thirty seconds checking me out and discard me as someone not worth knowing, but she didn't! From that morning we became best friends. Because of how smart and funny she was, people stopped ostracising me and I felt like I was welcomed into school more.

91

Both my mom and Jill, (my new friend's name), have told me that those possibilities were there all along I just didn't have the confidence before, but I think she was sent by an angel to rescue me.

I'm now twenty-one and have just finished college. I would like to say to all teenage girls who suffer from the same angst as I did that things will get better. Especially if you pray for it to happen.

Jana, 32

I have never seen an angel but I am very conscious of my guardian angel. I speak to her when I am in doubt about something, and I know that sometimes the voice of warning I hear in my head when I am getting into a risky situation is coming from her.

When I was young, I nearly died of a bad case of measles, and all the time I was lying in bed I felt that there was someone there watching me. I started to talk to her then and I know she helped me to pull through the illness. So from that day to this I have known that there is someone there looking after me. It is a good thing as we all need some help in life. People are weak and it is only because of God and the angels that we are able to be strong and to make good decisions.

Rico, 54

I am a runner. I regularly run half-marathons and I try to do a marathon at least once a year. When I am in training for a marathon, my regular daily runs vary from five to ten to fifteen miles, depending on the time available and where I am in my training regime.

When you run in a race it is quite a lonely experience, even though you are surrounded by other people. You are not really competing against the other runners. You are just trying to beat your personal target time, so it doesn't matter whether people pass you or you pass them. Occasionally you might exchange a few words of encouragement, though by the time you hit that wall of pain at about twenty miles, everyone is in the same boat and there is not a lot of talking.

However lonely it can be in a race, it is nothing compared to training on your own. I'm not complaining about it. I quite like the solitude, to be honest, but you are completely alone with your thoughts and when you get into the rhythm of running you almost move beyond conscious thought.

It is in those times that I have sometimes felt that I am communicating with angels. I found that if I talked to myself, sometimes it felt as though an answer was coming back to me from somewhere beyond my mind. So I concentrated on trying to slow my mind down, thinking about nothing but the next step, so it became almost a trance, like when you meditate. Then I would think about one thing only and see whether a voice came back to me.

For instance I thought once about "what are the good things in my life." And a voice came back to me. Sometimes it told me things about my life. Sometimes it asked questions about how I felt about the people in my life and the things I did.

It sounds a bit strange, I know, but I came to feel that as I ran there was an angel there with me. That was one of the only times my mind was quiet and uncluttered enough to allow me to hear his voice when he talked to me. Even in the middle of the night I find my mind is always racing with thoughts about the next day, memories, and strange ideas. But when I run on my own, I get into a very particular state of mind when I am thinking of almost nothing.

When I articulate a thought in my mind it is like throwing a stick out into a river and watching it slowly float away. And sometimes an answer comes back. I don't always hear that voice, though sometimes I think it is because I ask the wrong questions. Unless I am being completely honest in the thoughts I send out, I don't get an answer.

I suppose the other thing is that when I run I am going through quite a painful, difficult experience, so it is good to know that there is a spirit there with me, helping me to cope with the pain. In races I never hear that voice, but I still feel better for knowing that there might be an angel out there with me.

Lana, 28

I sometimes see an angel watching my twins. They are nine months old and were born prematurely. They didn't have to be in an incubator or anything, they were perfectly healthy. But they were tiny, and I have always worried about them. They are my first children. It is such a strange moment when the nurse at the hospital tells you that you can take them home.

Me and my partner looked at each other in shock – we had read all the books of course, but somehow it doesn't prepare you for that moment when they give you a real living human being (or two in my case) and tell you that you have to go away and look after them. If anything you want to stay in the hospital for longer just so you don't have to face up to the responsibility.

Then you get home and you have so much to worry about. Are you feeding them right? Is it OK if they sleep that way round? Every little cough or burp makes you concerned. And then you get no sleep because there is always one of them awake – they don't co-ordinate night-time sleeping unfortunately. They seemed to take it in turns to wake us up, every hour or so, on top of all the worry you are severely sleep-deprived.

Gradually, they started to sleep a little longer. But that doesn't help to start with because if you don't get woken up by them, you wake up in a panic that they have died in their sleep. Cot death is such a scary idea. We had a baby monitor in the bedroom, but often I would just end up lying down on the floor in their bedroom so I could be close to them.

It was one night when I was in there like that, that I first saw the angel. I opened my eyes, suddenly scared because I couldn't hear them breathing.

There was a man at the end of the bed. He had a very kind of face. It was a bit like you'd imagine a ghost looking, he was there but you could see the wall behind him. He just smiled at me and put his fingers on his lips. So I sat up quietly and looked in the cots and, of course, they were there, sleeping happily like two little angels.

I looked up to smile back at the angel. He kind of faded away as I was looking at him, but I understood he was still there. I lay back down on the floor and went back to sleep and the next I knew it was morning and my husband was there with two bottles ready for the twins.

That was the clearest view I had of the angel, but I have caught a glimpse of him once or twice since, and sometimes when I look down at my little babies I see them looking over my shoulder and smiling, and I just know he is there behind me looking down on them.

Peter, 64

I sometimes see two angels in church, behind the preacher. No-one else in the congregation seems to be able to see them. I'm not sure that they are there for the preacher himself. I'm not saying he isn't a good man, he is. But it always seems to me that the angels are there watching over all of us who are gathered there.

While other people bow their heads to pray or kneel, I tend to watch the back of the church to see if they are there. Sometimes I see them, sometimes I don't. But I feel that there is something about the group of people there all trying to commune in the sight of God that brings them to observe, listen and, perhaps, to be ready to intervene if we need them.

Cerys, 66

When my daughter was about twelve she used to be dreadfully embarrassed by me when we were out in public. Occasionally, that was my fault as I had the odd day when I had a drink too many and would behave a bit strangely. But then there were many other days when I was just being myself and she would be hideously embarrassed around me.

It used to set her off when I stopped to talk to people on the way down the high street. I'm naturally extrovert and she was quite a quiet child. She hated it when I stopped to talk to friends or acquaintances and would shrink away if I tried to introduce her. I did my best to try and find a happy medium and just to have a quick chat, but even then she would be cringing in the background, desperate for me to end the conversation and take her home.

She got over this in the end and turned out to be quite gregarious herself, but the thing I want to tell you about happened when she was still in that period when she saw me as an embarrassment.

She was old enough to cross the road on her own. It used to make me nervous when she did it, but I had to admit that she was doing it all very carefully and sensibly and I don't like to try and make children feel any more young and helpless than they are, so I had decided to let her cross the road on her own if she wanted.

One day she decided that the best way to get down the high street was for her to cross over to the other side and walk without me. That way, I could talk to people on my side of the road, while she would be on the other side, keeping an eye on me and staying within eye contact, but not having to be involved in the conversations. She would loiter on the other side of the road, pretending to look in shop windows and finding other ways to keep herself busy, I would chat to friends, and we were both happy that way.

I felt a bit strange about it. On the one hand I was proud of her for being so independent and resourceful, and for growing up and learning to find her own way in life. On the other hand I still saw her as my little baby and it made me anxious that she was separating herself from me in that way.

One day it was drizzling slightly, but still slightly sunny. There was a rainbow coming out in the sky. She was doing her thing of loitering on the other side of the road while I talked to a friend of our family that I had met. I looked over at her and saw an angel standing straight behind her, looking down on her. It was obviously an angel. It was a white figure, shining slightly in the rain and I felt a great feeling of calm and happiness as soon as I saw her.

I started to watch out for the angel, and a couple of times after that I saw her, though never quite as clearly as the first time. I tended to see her out of the corner of my eye, just a quick glance while I was talking to someone. If I tried to look straight at her, I didn't see the angel, but I came to realise that she was always there looking after her.

My feeling is that the angel had always been there for her, long before I caught a glimpse of her. It was just that at that time, when my daughter was starting to take her first steps away from me and find her own way in the world, she was at her most vulnerable and in the most need of being looked after. I like to think the angel is still there for her now, though I have no way of knowing that.

Finally, I'd like to tell you that my daughter now is pretty much my best friend. She still remembers those days when she used to walk on the other side of the road and we can make jokes about it. She probably still has the odd moment when she finds me embarrassing, but she is a proper grown up now. In fact she is almost middle aged, older than I was back in the period I have been telling you about.

It's strange how time passes and you suddenly realise that you are older than people you used to think were boring or ancient. I suppose I'm almost an "old lady" though I don't see myself that way at all. I still myself as the same girl I was back then, with a shy twelve-year-old watching me from the other side of the road.

Stephen, 43

Once, about ten years ago, I was tempted to use a prostitute. I was in Berlin on business. The red light district there is very brash, with big houses that are lit up. I'd walked past them a few times and been vaguely curious. I was married, but like most men I occasionally wondered what it would be like to try something different.

I had a meal with some business acquaintances and on the way back, on a whim, I went into one of the doorways to look around. It was quite strange. It smelt of incense, and there were just these corridors leading past doorways in which women were waiting for business, many of them dressed in very provocative outfits.

Most of them seemed a bit depressing or old but there were a few who were genuinely attractive and who even seemed quite friendly and nice although of course they would be like that to try and win some business.

I walked around, politely declining their advances, and went back to my hotel room. But once I was there I had a couple of beers from the minibar and started to convince myself that really it would be a one-off, harmless thing if I went back and paid one of the girls for sex.

At about two in the morning, slightly drunk, I decided

that I would regret it if I didn't, so I set off, with just my hotel keys and a few banknotes in my pocket. (Shamefully I had taken my wedding ring off and left it behind – something that shows the level of self-deception and shame I had sunk to.)

When I reached the red light district, I went back to the same building I had been to earlier. I looked up at the windows, which were lit up with pink neon.

There was a girl at one of the windows wearing a white dress. She was looking down at me with a face of such sadness that I hesitated. I suddenly thought about what I was doing and how I must look to those girls. Just another punter desperate to abuse their desperation.

I looked up at the girl again and she raised her eyebrows at me, as though she was asking me what I was going to do. I'm not arrogant enough to claim that an angel came to me especially to stop me making a mistake, but it is a strange thing in retrospect. In general those windows were set up so that you couldn't see through them, and it is peculiar that she was wearing white. And there was something about the whole way she looked at me that combined pity, disapproval and a deeper understanding.

Whoever she was, I felt she had seen into my soul, and it was a dark place at that moment. I turned around and set off back to the hotel. I put my wedding ring back on and I swear I haven't taken it off since. I didn't immediately know that I had made the right choice – I was going through a slightly difficult time with my wife at the time. But looking back I absolutely know I did the right thing. I would never have been able to shake off the shame if I had gone into that building that night.

Now I have two daughters. They are both young, but I think it gives me another way of looking at these things. Those poor girls are someone's daughter. I wish we lived in a world where there was no such thing as a red light district.

Emily, 77

I have several grandsons who are all grown up to be big strapping men now. But I never had a granddaughter. Until my youngest son remarried.

He had been married before, but his wife left him, It was all quite sad. I had never been sure that I liked her, but I had got used to her and he was very happy with her. Then suddenly she was gone and he was left grieving the marriage. She ran off with a man she had met at work.

They didn't have children. I'd never call that a blessing, but at least there was no custody problems. He was in his early forties at this stage and to be honest, I never expected him to have a child. But one day to my great surprise, he came and told me that he was going to be a father. I didn't even know he had a girlfriend.

She turned out to be a lovely girl called Jane, a few years younger than him. They had only been together for two or three month. They had been keeping it low key so that they could get to know each other, and were just considering going to meet each other's families when she found out that she was pregnant. So, of course, at that point they couldn't really put it off any more.

I was so pleased for him, and happy that he had found someone he loved. It could have been a disaster, going from a casual relationship to being parents so quickly, but they really seem to be soul mates. As soon as I met her I knew that they would be a good, strong couple. I only wished he had met her first, before the marriage that failed.

So now, eight years later, I have a beautiful grand-daughter, Lola. She is so wonderful, I can't even tell you. She is funny, clever and so full of energy. I live about a hundred miles away so I don't see her quite as much as I would like, but whenever I can I go to look after her, to give them a break, and she spends the odd weekend or week with me. I probably dote on her and spoil here a bit, but what can you expect? She deserves it.

Last month I took her to the cemetery near to my house while she was staying with me. I thought she would find it boring, but she became fascinated. There are all sorts of graves with angels, statues and inscriptions on them. She started reading about all the people who had died in the past and asking questions about them. Some were just little children, even younger than her and it had never occurred to her that children could die.

I explained that in the past there were illnesses that killed people that we can now cure and that cheered her up a bit. Then she started to ask me about how old people die. I know she doesn't really think of me as an old person, but every day I feel a little bit older, so it was a difficult thing to talk about. I explained how we all die in the end and the most important thing is to live a good life while you can. She seemed happy with that and ran off to look for squirrels in the trees.

I managed to hold off the tears until she was on her way across the graveyard. I wasn't crying for myself. I was crying because I know I won't live to see her grow up. I might make it until she is a teenager if I am lucky, or at the very best into her twenties. But I almost certainly won't meet her husband or her children or know her when she is properly grown up.

And the chances are she will not be as close to me when she is a teenager as she is now. So in that respect I suppose I was feeling sorry for myself. But on the whole I was just feeling a grief for not being able to be there for her for as long as I would want to. And I worry about the fact that she is probably going to stay an only child. It seems to me she might be lonely as she gets older.

As I was thinking about these things, she turned back from the bushes across the graveyard and started walking back to me.

I saw very clearly an angel walking behind her. The angel was a woman about the age of Lola's mother, Jane. She was dressed in white and had the most beautiful face I have ever seen. She looked at Lola and then looked at me and gave me a big smile.

I knew that she was letting me know that even if I couldn't always be there for Lola, there would always be someone there who loved her. And I realised that there will always be friends who love her, and she will eventually have a family of her own. I hope that when she is my age she remembers me with fondness, but there are more important things in the world than how she thinks about me.

Even though I still feel sad about the fact that I won't always be here, seeing that angel made a big difference to me. I know that even though I can't always be here, there is an angel beside her.

Connor, 26

When I first started nursery as a kid, I was terrified of leaving my parents and going off with all those strange kids.

For the first few days I was really unhappy, and at night I would find it hard to get to sleep. My mother used to try and reassure me. I think she got a bit tired of me telling her I couldn't sleep.

She came in and talked to me in the dark. She told me there was an angel who always watched over me while I was sleeping. She said she could see the angel at that moment at the end of the bed, and that the angel came to school with me in the morning, too.

She told me it was a woman with white wings and a lovely face and that you could see the light around the edge of her. She said the woman was smiling as she talked and nodding. Now, I know my mother was just trying to calm me down and give me something positive to think about when I was frightened.

However, I kept that image in mind and after that when I felt the first pangs of fear, I would imagine that kind angel standing there watching me to make sure nothing bad happened. In school I would imagine her standing in the corner of the room.

It made a huge difference to me. I soon calmed down at school and settled in, and I didn't really need any protection, but it was a soothing thought.

To this day when I am going through a bad time, I find it comforting to imagine an angel looking after me. If I wake in the dead of night and find worries or fears are keeping me awake, I think about that angel standing at the end of my bed, and it soothes me.

Lara, 39

I know that there are always angels beside us as we go through life, whether or not we see them or are directly aware of them. I am always conscious that the angels are there. They aren't just guardians. They are also there as witness to the good and bad deeds we do in life. If you are ever tempted to go down the path of bad acts, you should remember that there is an angel at your shoulder and that they are saddened by all the bad choices we make.

In my life I have made many bad choices. For a while in

my teens I used to shoplift. I also delivered drugs for a boyfriend of mine who sold cannabis, something I am not at all proud of.

On both occasions the thing that finally made me mend my ways was the idea that the angels were watching me and weeping as they saw the bad things I was doing.

From my more recent past I can tell you some more positive things. I got married five years ago and I am sure that the angels would be proud of me for choosing a good man and committing myself to him.

I also have two young children. At each birth I was very conscious of the angels smiling down at me as they saw those innocent, tiny babies. There is nothing more pure and beautiful in the entire world than a newborn baby.

As they grow older I will teach them about wrong and right and the ways of God. But I think the most important thing I will be able to communicate to them is the certain knowledge that we live among the angels.

Messengers

It seems that angels sometimes take the role of messenger. In these accounts people receive messages from loved ones who have died or who are in peril, from strangers and from spirits in another realm.

Traditionally, angels were known as beings who could travel between the spiritual and material realm, and so were one of the few ways in which messages could be passed between the two. Of course, there are also circumstances, even in this age of global communication, when we are unable to get an important message to our friends or family and here we also find accounts where angels have chosen to carry a message from one person to another within our world.

Marco, 28

I heard about my father's death from an angel.

Actually that's not quite true. This is what happened. I was away at college and my father had been ill for some time with throat cancer. However, he seemed to be responding to treatment and we all hoped he was going to recover.

One day, I was in the marketplace looking at some clothes on a stall when someone tapped me on the shoulder. It was a man I had never seen before. He said to me that my father wanted me to know I shouldn't worry about him and had sent a message that I should "be myself and be happy". Then the man just smiled and walked away.

It was pretty crowded in the marketplace and when I tried to follow him, I lost him in the crowd.

I don't know why, but I just knew that this meant something bad had happened. I pretty much ran all the way back to my room to call home. I spent about fifteen minutes trying to call my home, but the line was constantly busy.

Then there was a knock on my door. It was my sister. She had got up at dawn to drive to the town where I lived. As soon as she opened the door I said, "It's dad, isn't it?" She just nodded and started crying. I told her I'd been trying to call, and led her inside and sat her down. He had died the night before and she had come as soon as she could as they felt it was best if someone could tell me in person rather than phoning. They had left the phone off the hook on purpose so I couldn't call.

Later, she asked me how I knew. Obviously, her turning up on my doorstep without warning could have given me a clue, but as she said, it was like I was expecting her, and seemed unexpectedly calm about it.

In fact, I think she was a bit disappointed, in a strange way, that I wasn't more shocked. It seemed at the time as though I was being callous because I didn't react with shock and tears. I did, of course, cry later when no-one was around – sometimes it takes a while for the shock of someone dying to really hit you.

But in this case it was more than that – I really did feel that I had had a message from him that reached me soon after his death. I had never really believed in angels before that, but it is something that I can't explain in any other way.

Jane, 45

When my daughters first started going out on their own as teenagers, I was always worried about their safety. They had mobile phones and instructions to phone home if there were any problems, but you know what teenage girls are like. They think they know everything and you are just being stupid for worrying.

For the most part, I have to say they did prove to be quite sensible, so to some degree my worries were perhaps excessive. But there was one time when something bad could easily have happened.

My youngest daughter, Josie, had gone to a house party. I assumed it would be the usual kind of thing, a fairly chaotic affair, but it was only a few streets away and Josie had her phone.

I was on the sofa watching the television at about 11 o'clock. She was not due home until midnight and, given the way that they push the boundaries, I was expecting her any time between then and half past midnight. I closed my eyes for a moment and I heard a very clear voice saying "Josie needs you."

Of course, I opened my eyes and looked around. I even ran outside to see if there was someone out there, but there was no sign of anyone.

I thought I might have imagined it, but I didn't want to risk it. So I grabbed my car keys and ran to the car and drove round to the house where the party was taking place. I knew that if there was nothing wrong she would be furious but I couldn't ignore that voice.

I went into the party ignoring all the teenagers who glared at me as an intruding adult. I have to say it was one of the worst messes I have ever seen. There was a stench of cannabis (I'm not an innocent about these things, but it does make me worry when drugs are being used so flagrantly). There was a boy passed out in the front garden and smashed glass all over the hall floor. If I had been the parents of the child holding the party I would have been furious.

I was only worried about finding Josie, though. No-one seemed to be able to tell me where she was. I managed to find her best friend, who was quite drunk but managed to point me towards the back garden.

I couldn't see her there, though there were a few kids sitting around talking and drinking. It was luck that I bothered to check the shed at the very end. To start with someone seemed to be holding the door shut. Then I shoved it open and saw Josie on the floor, seemingly unconscious. Her shirt was partially undone and there were three boys in there looking very guilty.

Then Josie stirred and saw me and reached out for me. The boys shoved past me and ran away. She was slurring her words and only just able to keep her eyes open, but she was really relieved and grateful to see me. I got her on her feet and managed to lead her to the car and drove her home.

The full story took a while to come out. She had had a few drinks, and there was a boy she liked. But it seems as though either he or one of his friends had put something in her drink and she suddenly found herself going very woozy and strange. The boys first offered to help, by taking her outside for fresh air but then they made her go into the shed. Anything could have happened if she had been left alone in there with them in that state and none of her friends had bothered to look after her properly.

I complained to the parents and the police and made as much fuss as I could. But the thing I really cared about was that I had managed to get there and keep her safe. She didn't really see those people any more after that – it was the last month before she went away to college anyway, and she was quite shocked at what had nearly happened.

In the end I think it did her some good. She is a sensible child really and she had just been a bit too careless and trusting. I pray that she has learned from the experience. But I also give thanks every day to that voice that warned me that she needed me.

Tom, 72

My wife died ten years ago. She was younger than me and, if I'm honest, I'd always assumed I'd die first, so it came as a surprise to find myself left here without her after she went, before I had even had a chance to retire to spend more time with her.

I go to her grave several times a week. She isn't actually buried there. It is a family grave, and she was cremated, so I scattered the ashes there and we added a small stone for her.

I treat it as her grave, though, and that is where I go when I feel like talking to her. I tell her about all the little things in my life, how people she knows are getting on, the trouble I've been having working out how the washing machine works, all those kinds of things.

I don't hear her talking back to me, but I can imagine the kinds of things she would say. And often I enjoy having those little chats, it cheers me up to remember her and to think about how she would laugh to see me trying to work out how the dishwasher works.

Sometimes I get sad, too. One time I was down there telling her about her new granddaughter Jay. She was born two years after my wife died, and she never had the chance to meet her. She is a beautiful little thing, and would have made her grandmother so proud.

I choked up telling her about it, and stood there crying. I started telling her how much I missed her, and how I hated having to do everything without her.

Then I felt a warm hand on my shoulder and someone told me, "She misses you, too. But you have to love Jay for her." I even felt breath on my cheek, but I didn't open my eyes. It felt wrong, somehow.

I leant on the grave and when I opened my eyes I was alone there, but I really felt like I had been given a message. It is the only time since she died that I really realised that she was there watching me all the time, and would be there for me when my time eventually came. It was a weight off my shoulders.

She was right, too – she can't be here to see her grandchildren growing older, so I have to give them love from both of us and do my best to tell them about her so that they know what a wonderful woman their grandmother was.

Willow, 25

I have only vague memories about this because I was very young when it happened but my mother has told me about it. When I was about five or six years old, I was sleeping in a very old bed which had been in the family for over a hundred years. It was about the same height as a hospital bed with a sturdy wrought iron frame.

Apparently, I used to talk to a young man at night when I was in bed. My mother and father had separated when I was only eighteen months old and my mum was curious who I was talking to because no one was in the room with me. After checking on me, she disregarded the whole incident thinking that I was perhaps playing with dolls or something.

She thought it a bit strange when it happened again. I was clearly talking to someone, having a conversation rather than making something up as I went along. My mother told me that before long I was having conversations with this man every night when I went to bed. Mum eventually asked who the man was and she told me that I told her that he was someone who had died a long time ago. She was confused and told me not to be silly and to stop talking to this man at night.

Around this time I have memories of waking up at night and seeing a man standing by my bed. He was very pale, almost transparent as if lit only by ultra-violet light. I don't remember what our conversations were about but I do remember thinking at the time that he was an angel. One morning I woke up in hospital. My mum told me that I had rolled out of bed and cracked my skull open. I wonder now whether the man had come to warn me. It was a very serious injury and I was lucky not to have been affected long term or even killed.

I now believe that children are more open-minded and maybe that's why I could see the man and my mum couldn't.

Ally, 36

One of my best friends, Ellie, told me she was getting married when we were twenty-five. I was really shocked and I didn't like her boyfriend much. I didn't think I'd reacted badly, I was a bit shocked but I congratulated her. And then later on I made some silly joke about how her children would have his big ears.

Apparently that was the thing that really upset her. She had always thought I didn't like him much and this proved it. That much I heard from my other friends afterwards. They told me she'd been upset later that night and had felt like I wasn't really pleased about her engagement. But I thought she'd get over it.

Then things got a bit weird. She stopped talking to me and told everyone I wasn't coming to the wedding because I didn't want to. I was angry at her because this wasn't true. At least it wasn't totally true. But she was right in some ways. I was shocked that she was getting married. It seemed so irrevocable, and made me feel old. And I'd never liked Pete, her boyfriend, much, so that didn't help.

My immediate reaction was to just accept that we had fallen out, and for a month or two we didn't talk. Our friends tried to persuade me to talk to her but I was feeling offended by the way she behaved.

Then on the night of her hen night (which of course I didn't go to) I had a dream. An angel came to talk to me. It was a really proper angel, a lovely woman with big white wings and a shining light all around her. She talked to me about how I was feeling about Ellie. In the dream I was crying and crying because I was so upset we had fallen out, even though that wasn't how I was behaving in real life. And then she talked to me about what kind of friends we were.

I remembered all these little things from school, like when I was being bullied and she had sided with me even though no one else had, and when we had first gone to a club and she had looked after me when I drank too much. And how I'd helped her when she was going through her dieting fad and had been heartbroken by her first boyfriend.

The angel was very calm and didn't tell me what to do. She just made me think about what I was throwing away. When I woke up I was still crying. My cheeks were wet and my throat was sore, like I had actually been crying in my sleep.

I called her up right that moment. Even though it was five in the morning. It didn't actually go that well. She wasn't best pleased to be woken at that time, though I did at least tell her I was sorry and wanted to go to the wedding, which was only a couple of days later.

That afternoon I got an invitation, at last. She had couriered it to me at work to make sure I got it, which made me feel more optimistic. I didn't actually manage to speak to her before the ceremony. I didn't want to bother her because I knew she'd be busy. But I bought a lovely dress and a present and promised myself not to be upset by the fact I wasn't a bridesmaid.

The wedding was amazing, lots of lovely people and food and friends. I talked to her a little bit during the meal and though it was a bit strained, it was clear that we were going to be OK.

After she had danced with Pete that evening I made sure I had a dance with him myself, then I sat with him for a little while to chat and realised how wrong I'd been. He was so in love with her and so proud that she had agreed to be his wife, it was immediately obvious he was going to be great with her.

I think that's what won her round in the end. When she realised I'd made my peace with Pete she came and gave me a big hug and finally we had a laugh and a bit of a cry about it all. (We didn't spend all night talking – we left that until a few weeks later when we had our own little hen night and talked about all the awkward things we hadn't mentioned at the wedding and I finally managed to talk about why I'd been such an idiot about it all.)

So in the end it all worked out for the best. We're still really good friends. I've got kids now and we are in and out of each others' houses all the time. She's been a brilliant friend. I suppose a psychologist might say the angel came from my unconscious or my conscience or whatever. Whether it came from there or somewhere much more mysterious I know it helped me when I needed it most.

Bill, 75

After my wife died I used to have dreams where an angel came to me and gave me notes from her. They were written out in her careful longhand.

They weren't always about anything important. Sometimes she talked about things we had done when we were younger, funny stuff she remembered. Other times she would ask me if I was eating properly and remind me to lock the windows when I went out. Silly things, exactly the same sorts of things she would have been talking about if she had been there.

I remember one letter when she told me how she still remembered every detail of our wedding. She told me a story about how my cousin had drunk too much and fallen asleep in a corner of the scout hall where we had the reception. I'd completely forgotten that until I read it in that letter. But she did also tell me how much she missed me and loved me and that was a good thing to hear.

I still write her letters, too. I know it's silly, but I think if I write a letter and put it into the biscuit tin where we always used to keep letters from family, the angel might take it back to her. I won't tell you everything I write to her about. A lot of it is the same kinds of little things she writes to me about. But I can tell you that I make sure to tell her I love her and miss her, too.

Sally, 42

I'm always appalled by the way young people drive. They seem to have no consideration for others, or even fear or understanding of the risks they are taking with their own lives. And, of course, sometimes it is themselves who they hurt through this carelessness.

Anna, a friend of mine who lives in the country was recently woken up by a frantic banging at her door. There was a woman there, looking distraught. She asked if she could use the phone to call the emergency services to report an accident. Anna heard her telling the operator that there were three people still alive and that one had been thrown into the woods. She went upstairs to throw some clothes on as she thought she might be needed at the scene.

The woman was already leaving as she got downstairs, so she grabbed her keys and followed her. From her house it is about a five minute walk down the lane to the main road, or less if you run, which she did.

The funny thing was that it was just after she left the

house that she heard the sound of a car crash. There was a shriek of brakes, then two loud bangs. A few moments after that, she saw a ball of flames through the trees.

She ran faster and arrived to a terrible scene. Two cars had left the road, one was upside down in a field and in flames. If anyone was in there they would certainly be dead. The other had crashed through a fence and into some trees. The woman was nowhere to be seen. As she was taking this in and trying to work out what to do, an ambulance arrived. It was literally a minute or so after the crash, even though it is over five minutes to the town. Then the police arrived and all the emergency workers started running around . She asked if she could help but they said it would be best if she let them get on with it.

Afterwards a policeman came to the house to take her details and to find out if she had seen the crash. She explained the situation. She asked him what had happened, and explained that she had heard the crash after the woman had arrived at her house and called them. At that point she still thought there must have been more than one accident, an earlier one which then caused the one she had heard. He told her that there were only two vehicles involved and that they had rescued three survivors, all teenagers from the other car. The driver of the car in the field was dead, probably on impact. They hadn't done their investigations of course, but it appeared that one or both cars had simply been taking the bend too far out and too fast and then they had either lost control or glanced off each other and gone off the road.

Obviously, Anna followed the news reports afterwards. She was struck by something in the newspaper. The officer in charge of the case was reported as thanking the anonymous person who had phoned them because she had told them about a third teenager, a girl. She had been thrown through the windscreen and was hidden deep in some bushes, with bad cuts and some broken bones. The officer said that she would have been likely to die without the prompt medical treatment she received, so the call that had been made had probably saved her life.

It was this, combined with the mystery of how the woman had arrived to make that call before the crash even happened, that convinced Anna that something spiritual had happened. I'm sceptical about these things, but I have to admit I can't find any other explanation than that an angel or spiritual being chose to save that young girl.

When you see and hear about things like that, it makes you really think about why we are here and why we take our existence so lightly. Really, we should thank God every day for our lives and make sure we don't waste the short time we are given here.

Barry, 38

My eldest son, Gary, went off on a gap year last year. He was doing the full round-the-world travelling thing, down through the US to South America, then from Australia up to South East Asia.

I mostly don't worry about him. He's a sensible lad and I trust his judgment. However, one night I had a dream where an angel told me that I had to get in touch with him. It was very much how you would imagine an angel looking, beautiful with a shining light around them – I wasn't sure if it was a man or a woman, it seemed to be something completely different.

When I woke up I immediately started trying to track Gary down. He hadn't updated his Facebook page for a few days, and I wasn't getting any signal from his mobile.

Eventually I managed to track down one of the friends who was with him. It turned out that he had been arrested for brawling in Rio and thrown in this unpleasant jail. They hadn't wanted to bother us parents about it – they didn't have the money to pay a fine so Gary was stuck inside for three weeks.

Of course, I was furious with him for trying to cover this up. I wired the money for the fine that day (he will be paying me back next year, don't worry…) I managed to talk to him later. He said it wasn't his fault, and I believe him. He had just got caught up in this fight between two Dutch kids and somehow the police ended up taking him in as well.

He hadn't wanted to worry me, but I hate to think how he'd have coped in there. Apparently it was pretty tough and as soon as he had spent the first night there he was really regretting not getting in touch but had no way of contacting me.

He went on with his travels but I made him promise never to hide anything like that again. It still worries me to think of him out there on his own. I suppose the only consolation is that he is so grown up that he thinks he can cope with something like that alone. But, honestly, you would prefer that they thought of themselves as kids and remembered to ask for help when they really need it.

Helen, 22

After my mother died, my father went through a period of drinking way too much. I was fifteen and my sister was eleven at the time. It was pretty horrible for me, because I was trying to come to terms with the idea that she had gone, yet I ended up having to act almost as a mother to my sister. I kept asking him not to drink so much, but he told me I didn't understand.

We would talk in quite a sensible way about it, and he would tell me how much he missed my mum and how proud he was of us. And then he'd just go and get drunk again anyway, and I'd be stuck trying to get my sister to bed on time, and get her up for school. Then I'd have to sort out all the shopping and laundry. And finally I had to worry about whether my dad had left the oven on and the front door unlocked when he fell asleep in a drunken stupor on the floor. This was all on top of whether he was going to end up hurting himself or drinking himself to death. At least twice I had to take car keys off him when he was drunk and wanted to drive to the shop for more beer. And all the while my school work was suffering.

This was pretty much my daily routine and I was becoming exhausted and depressed. I was also angry at him. I knew how unhappy he was, but I really needed him to hold it together and look after us. I wanted someone to look after me for a change.

One night I was lying in bed waiting for him to come home from the bar where he was drinking. Instead of feeling angry, I was feeling absolutely miserable, and I remember praying for someone to help me with him.

At about one in the morning I heard him coming through our garden gate. Instead of the usual rattle of keys as he fumbled with the lock, there wasn't any more noise for a few minutes. I went to the window and saw him lying on the grass in the front garden. There was a woman I had never seen before kneeling next to him. I could her lips moving as she talked to him.

I went down to see what the problem was. Once I got out there the woman was gone and he was sitting up looking drunkenly around. I gave him a hand and helped him up the steps. There was no point in shouting at him as he would only be too drunk to listen to me.

I remember he did have an odd expression on his face that night. He was looking around at everything with a kind of wonder. He looked a bit like a child on the morning of Christmas Day, when everything is exciting and new.

To my amazement, he was the first one up the next day. He had already made breakfast when he brought me a cup of tea to wake me up. He mumbled an apology about being home late, then drove us to school. He seemed very subdued.

That day he cleaned the house from top to bottom. He did all the laundry and ironing that had been piling up. He stocked up the freezer and the fridge with food. And instead of me heating up something out of the freezer for our dinner he made a proper stew like my mother used to make.

He was still very quiet, but after my sister got to bed he sat me down in the front room and gave me a tearful apology for all the times he had got drunk and behaved badly. I was so happy I just gave him a big hug and started crying. For the first time since the funeral I felt like a little girl being looked after by her parent instead of having to be the grown-up one.

He didn't touch a drop of alcohol for the rest of that year. Today he does have the occasional glass of wine, but he has moved on a long way from where he was after my mother died. We are all still sad about losing her, but from that night he went back to being my father and being someone I could respect, instead of a drunken fool crawling on the floor.

It was a couple of years before he told me the full story. He said he had got home and fallen over on the grass in the front garden. He had decided he might as well sleep there, which was pretty stupid as it was a cold time of year.

Then he found a woman leaning over him. She whispered in his ear and told him how much he was hurting me. She told him how disappointed she was to see him being so selfish, and that he needed to be a proper father to me. She reminded him that however he behaved I would always remember it. But she also told him that my mother still loved us all, whatever we did.

Then the next thing he knew I was there, helping him to his feet. He told me that he had been a bit dazed by it all, and had suddenly felt overwhelmed by the memory of his love for my mother. Instead of feeling sorry for himself he was thinking about how lucky he was to have had the time he did with her and to have a family to look after. That was why he was looking round in a strange way.

He had been so worried he would forget all this, he'd stayed up all night, drinking a lot of water and writing it all down in his notebook. And the next day he'd vowed to make my mother proud of him and to look after us properly.

I always feel that the woman must have been an angel who either answered my prayer or came to bring him a message from my mother. Either way, it worked – that is the only period of my life when I haven't had full respect for him, and I forgave him for that lapse long ago. I always understood why he was doing it, I just needed him to be there for me, too.

Carla, 54

Angels bring me messages from my son, who died four years ago. He was only thirty, he was shot when he tried to intervene and save someone from being robbed on the street.

It was typical of him that instead of turning his back and ignoring the problem, he tried to help out, so while it was tragic that he was murdered, I think of his actions with pride.

Of course I miss him terribly. One day, about a month after his death, I woke up and there was the brightest light in my bedroom, filling the whole room with golden light.

An angel came out of the light to me and said that David wanted me to know he was fine and that I shouldn't be too sad. I tried to speak, to ask questions or send a message back, but I couldn't say anything. Then suddenly the light was gone and I was in the room alone.

The same thing has happened a few times, for different reasons. A month or two after that an angel came and told me David was worrying because I wasn't eating enough or getting enough sleep. It was true, I was still in mourning and I wasn't looking after myself. I'd almost seen it as a mark of respect to not look after myself, as it showed I didn't really care about myself more than my son who I had lost.

However, after that I realised that David wouldn't want to see me get ill for his sake. I started to eat properly and get some proper sleep and I felt a whole lot better.

Another time an angel was there when I woke up, just to tell me that David loved me. That was the one and only time I managed to speak. I told the angel I loved David, too. The angel just said "he knows."

Then last year I met a new man. David's father left when he was fifteen and we were very close to each other. In all those years I had been on a few dates, but I had never found the right man and had never felt like becoming part of a couple again. It was painful the first time I got divorced and I figure I didn't want to go through that again.

However, Sam seemed different, he felt like a person I could spend the rest of my life with. But part of me was resisting falling in love with him. I think it was that same bit of me that had felt that eating or sleeping properly when my son was dead would be self-indulgent. Now I felt that moving on with my life, to a new relationship or even marriage would be moving away from my son. And I was scared to do that.

So again, I woke to find an angel in my room. And all he said was that David thought I could be happy with Sam, and nothing would make him happier than to see me with a good man.

I got married to Sam last year and I couldn't be any prouder or happier. I will always miss David, but I know he is there in my heart and Sam understands that, too.

Caroline, 25

My grandmother died in 2008 and it has taken me a long time to come to terms with losing her. We were very close. My sister and my mother were at the hospital with her when she died but I was working a late shift and wasn't able to be there. I was upset by that, too and I didn't even get to say goodbye to her in her casket.

A month or so after she died I had a dream about my grandmother. She was lying in her coffin and there were some people I didn't recognise messing with her. I tried to pull them away and felt a tap on my shoulder. When I turned around it was my grandma standing behind me.

She was wearing a blue dress that she wore all the time and looked much healthier than at the end of her life. She said, "Don't worry, that's not me." Then she gave me a big hug and I started to cry. My grandmother told me not to cry because we'd be together again one day. She told me that she was alright and wiped away my tears just like she used to when I was a child. She told me that an angel was waiting for her and that it was beautiful where she was now.

I told my mother about the dream and about the blue dress. She told me that they had buried her in that dress because it was the one she was most comfortable in. I had thought they had put her in her 'best' blouse and skirt but they had changed their minds at the last minute. I couldn't have known that.

I think that my grandmother came to me in the dream to let me know she was OK. When she told me that it wasn't her in the coffin she meant that she wasn't a dead body any more but a spirit in heaven.

Guardian Angels

Another of the traditional roles of angels is as guardians. It seems most common to find accounts of guardian angels intervening to look after young children. It has always seemed to me that angels have the most connection with children because of their innocence. And it may also be that children still have open minds and so are able to sense angels around them or to communicate with them more easily than adults, who have become hardened by life and have set ideas about what is possible and impossible.

Of course, there are also adults who still feel the presence of their guardian angels or who have clear memories of angels from their own childhood. So it is not that only children have guardian angels. But perhaps they are more in need of someone to look after them than grown ups, who more frequently have to take responsibility for their own mistakes.

Caroline, 49

When my son was about eight months old I took him shopping at the local superstore. I always had difficulty with the pushchair. There are no elevators and a lot of staircases and I'm only 95 lbs, quite small. I decided to try going up the stairs backwards, pulling it up as I walked backwards. I had seen other moms doing this so wanted to give it a try.

I got about half way up when I felt myself slip. I remember my legs shooting out from under me and I let go of the pushchair and heard it clatter down the stairs. My son was still strapped in it and I was really frightened because I couldn't hear him cry. I thought he must be critically injured and struggled desperately to my feet.

As I stood up I could see the pushchair lying on its side but my son wasn't in it. He was completely OK and in the arms of the woman who'd been following me up the stairs. I rushed down the stairs and thanked her as I took my baby from her.

I did a quick examination of his face and body but he was cut and bruise-free. When I turned to thank the woman she had gone. I asked another lady where she had gone but she told me that she hadn't seen anyone other than me and my son.

Ever since that day I've wondered about it. My son is now in his twenties and completely healthy. I just can't see how, in the split second it took for the pushchair to fall, she could have got him out of the straps. I think that she could have been an angel who saved his life.

June, 54

I was in a nasty car crash when I was in my twenties. I broke a leg, a wrist and two ribs and also suffered a head injury. I stupidly wasn't wearing a seatbelt and that was the main reason I was hurt so badly.

I don't actually remember the crash. Apparently a driver coming towards me was overtaking and I lost control trying to evade him as he was about to crash into me headlong. I missed him but skidded off the road into a ditch and was thrown against the windscreen.

After that I was taken to hospital. But I didn't know that. Instead I remember being in a dark place I had never seen before. I realised that there were two angels there with me. I was walking along a long road and there was an angel either side of me. They were talking to me, encouraging me to keep walking.

I couldn't remember anything about who I was or where I was. However, one of the angels started to talk to me about my family. She told me about my mother and where I lived and slowly I started to remember fragments. She told me I had to remember if I wanted to get back there from the dark place.

Then the other angel spoke to me and said that it was too soon for me to die and that I had to try to keep breathing and to keep walking. It was terribly difficult. I wanted very badly to just lie down and go to sleep but he wouldn't let me. He was quite stern about it, and told me off every time I felt weak. And meanwhile the other angel kept telling me about my family and reminding me about how much they wanted to see me. And between them they kept me going while I walked down that dark road.

Then I saw a light doorway ahead of me and they told me to keep walking. I asked if I'd see them again and they just stopped walking and smiled. So I took a deep breath and kept on walking and then suddenly, like I was coming out of deep water into the daylight, I found myself in a white hospital room, wired up to all kinds of machinery.

I had been unconscious for two days. I woke up enough to see that my mother, brother and aunt were there talking to me, but I was very confused. I was on a drip and also on painkilling injections. To be honest, once I woke up and felt the pain, I just wanted to go back to that dark place and talk to the angels, but I knew I couldn't do that. And over the days and weeks I was stuck in there in the hospital I gradually got stronger and started to heal. My family were always there for me, of course, and I will never forget how hard they worked at looking after me for months afterwards.

It was a scary experience in many ways, but I also learnt a lot from it and feel grateful to know that there were angels there looking after us, even if it takes something as terrible as that for us to actually meet them here.

Jen, 32

I used to see my guardian angel when I was a child.

I was scared of the dark. I used to ask my mother to leave the bedroom light on because I was frightened of monsters under the bed. I had to tuck every part of my body under the sheets so that I knew nothing could reach out from under the bed and grab my foot or hand.

Gradually my mother started to refuse to leave even the little bedside lamp switched on. Then she gradually closed the bedroom door more each night so that I had a smaller crack of light coming into the room. And then at last came the day when she decided I was old enough to have the door closed and the lights off.

I'm sure she was doing the right thing, trying to gradually get me used to going to sleep in the dark. I don't hold it against her at all. I was still scared though, every night.

Then, one night, I looked down the bed in the dark, and as my eyes gradually became used to the light I saw a tall figure looking down at me. You would think that I would be scared, but this was something completely different. There was a very low light coming from the figure. I couldn't see the face clearly but I felt that this was a kind, calm presence. I relaxed slightly, feeling that she was there looking after me. And I fell asleep like that.

After that I always looked for her. Sometimes I could make her out; sometimes I couldn't be sure that she was there. But knowing about her always made me feel calmer as I tried to sleep. And somewhere along the way I forgot to be afraid of the dark.

I remember my mother asking me if I was OK, one day when she turned the light out. I told her I wasn't scared any more because of the guardian angel that looked after me. She paused to give me a strange look, and then smiled and we never mentioned it again.

Saffron, 24

This is a story that my older sister, Raffi, told me. It happened when my niece was a baby – she is now seven years old. My sister used to attend a computer class in the evening so as to improve her job prospects when her daughter went to school. She took her daughter with her as there were childcare facilities available.

During the winter it was dark when the classes ended and my sister didn't have a car so had to walk home. One of the streets she walked down was very quiet and she told me that she used to walk as fast as she could to get to the main road.

One night as she was walking home with her little girl, she realised that a man had stepped out of the bushes and was following her. He seemed intoxicated on something and began shouting abuse at her. She was very frightened and held her baby to her, (the baby was in a sling).

As she hurried, a man walking a dog passed her on the other side of the road. When he saw what was happening he crossed the road and began to walk with her. He told her not to be afraid and that he'd walk with her as far as her home if necessary. The man then began shouting abuse at the man with the dog.

After getting no response from either the man or my sister the abusive man eventually gave up and headed off. The man with the dog chatted with my sister and walked her all the way home. As she was unlocking her door she turned round to thank the man but there was nobody there.

She walked back down her path and looked up and down the road and the man and his dog had vanished. She told me that she believes that they had been specially sent to guide her and her little baby girl back home safely.

Beth, 31

My mom died when I was just nine years old and I dreaded the same thing happening to my son. He is now twenty years old but as a single parent I've been overly aware of danger and always tried to protect him.

There was an incident when he was eight years old where he came running into the house to tell me that he'd been racing with his friend and in his persistence to become the winner had tripped up and fell. He said that he could see broken glass on the floor and felt sure he was about to fall face first into it.

He waited for the impact, worrying that it might get into his eyes so he kept them shut tightly. Suddenly he told me that he was pulled back by two strong arms. The next thing he knew he was standing upright and there was no one there.

I'm sure it was his guardian angel that saved him. I remember another incident from when he was a tiny baby. His father was a very violent man and I had told him to leave. He had just moved out when I was sitting in the living room feeling emotional when I felt a presence standing in front of me. Initially I was a little afraid but the presence seemed to move closer and I felt wrapped in a warm glow.

The presence seemed to put its arms around me and then I heard a voice. It said only one thing, "courage", and I knew it was my mother, I could smell her perfume and I recognised her voice. I always wonder if she is the guardian angel.

Ali, 34

You see stories on the news about how people are left to die on city streets because no-one thinks to stop and check what has happened. The same thing nearly happened to me once.

I was in the city centre in the early evening when a mugger tried to grab my bag. I was down a side street but it wasn't a blind alley or anything. However, there was no-one around at that exact moment.

It was instinct that made me fight back and refuse to let go of the bag. I pushed him off and he fell back against the wall. I turned to run away and at that moment I felt a thump in my side and a kind of slap on the side of my head and I fell over, hitting my head again on the ground. From the sidewalk I saw him running away with my bag. But then I passed out.

I didn't know this at the time but he had stabbed me in the side with a blade then punched me on the side of my head. So I was there, bleeding on the ground and unconscious while he ran away.

The rest of the story comes from the man who saved me, who was called Peter B. He was walking down the street and saw me lying on the floor from a long way off. People were just walking past me. It was starting to get dark and perhaps people couldn't see that what I was lying in was my blood, but no-one stopped to check if I was in trouble. They just all assumed I was drunk or on drugs and stepped round me or crossed the road to get away. I can imagine doing the same myself at the time though I never would after what happened to me.

Peter B. was going to walk past me, too. He just assumed that people were ignoring me for a reason. He told me afterwards that he thought I had drunk too much and that if he tried to help I would just be sick on him or something. But just after he walked past me, someone grabbed him by the shoulders and told him to go back and help me. He said it was a woman dressed in perfectly ordinary clothes. He couldn't really describe her afterwards because it happened so fast. He turned to look at me, then back at the woman and, as fast as that, she had disappeared. He thought it very strange but he did at least decide to come and look at me, and suddenly realised I was bleeding, not intoxicated.

He put me in the recovery position and used his cell phone to call emergency. I was taken to the hospital and they did a great job. The wound was not that deep but if I had been left there for too much long I could easily have bled to death. So I owed Peter B. my life, but also the strange woman who stopped him and forced him to turn around.

I suppose the moral of the story is that if you see someone in trouble, please do stop and help. I know it is scary to get involved, but you never know when you might be in a position to save someone's life. I like to think that the strange woman was my guardian angel, but we can't always rely on angels to save us. Sometimes we need the help of a Good Samaritan as well.

Jimmy, 22

My grandfather lived with us in our family home from when I was nine years old. He had had a stroke and wasn't as mobile as he used to be. My dad had built a kind of separate studio apartment in an extension and that's where my grandfather lived. I remember one night when I was about fifteen, waking up to find him in my bedroom doorway. He said, "Alicia, I won't be here much longer but I want to tell you that I'm proud of you and love you very much." Then he disappeared. I presumed that he'd gone back to his apartment.

The next morning when I woke up I could hear crying downstairs. When I got down to the kitchen my mom was crying at the kitchen table. Immediately I knew what must have happened. I said, "It's granddad. He's died hasn't he?" My mom was a bit startled by the fact that I knew, I didn't say anything about my experience the night before in case she didn't believe me or it upset her.

Many years later, I eventually told my older brother about what had happened that night and he looked stunned and asked me if mom had ever told me anything about the night my granddad died. According to my brother, mom had been woken up that night by my grand-dad telling her that his time was up but he'd always look after her and the children. Then he turned around and there was an angel standing behind him smiling at my mother.

When she woke up the next morning she found my granddad dead when she took him his breakfast through as usual.

We think now that granddad had probably had another stroke and hadn't wanted us to call an ambulance to keep him alive too much longer. He had always loved riding his bicycle along the river and had been miserable since he couldn't get around independently any more. He was saying goodbye to us rather than be taken back to hospital.

Kathy, 22

I grew up in a children's home and when I was eighteen I left to live in a tiny council flat. The first night I spent alone there I was really scared and lonely. I sat on my bed with the lights on praying, then turned off the light and went to sleep. I awoke at exactly midnight and heard a voice calling my name.

I looked around and suddenly felt really warm and comforted. In the corner of the room there was a shape standing by my bed. As my eyes adjusted I saw that it was a man in a long white robe with huge wings at the back. In his hand he carried a very ornate sword that he lifted above his head. He smiled at me and then slowly disappeared.

When I woke up the next morning everything seemed different. I had been worrying so much about living alone with no one to look after me but I suddenly felt full of confidence.

I think I saw my guardian angel that night at a time in my life when I yearned for comfort. In the months that followed I enrolled myself in college and got a job to pay for my education. Four years later, I have a degree, a good job and a lovely boyfriend and I'm no longer lonely.

Megan, 24

I think that my baby daughter can see angels. She often sits on the floor looking up at the ceiling and smiling. She's been doing it since she learned to sit up. Sometimes she points and says, "Look."

The other day she lifted both arms like she does when she wants me to pick her up. It's as if she wants to get closer to whatever it is that she can see.

My mother sometimes comes to babysit and she has commented on this as well so it's not just me. The thing is that I'm really frightened that it means that she is going to die. My mother says it is just that my daughter can see her guardian angel and that is a good thing. I really hope so.

Harry, 29

When I was twenty-one I went diving in a local river with some of my friends. The river did get very deep in some parts and there could also be strong currents but we knew the river well and thought we'd be OK. I lost one of my flippers and went swimming after it. It was a very windy day and the recent heavy rain had made the currents flow very quickly. Before I knew it I was being swept along away from my friends.

I could feel myself being sucked downwards and I was struggling to fight my way back to the surface. It was hard to do with only one flipper. Suddenly, I felt an enormous sense of peace. I knew that I was about to drown but felt very happy. At this moment I felt someone pull me by my hand.

Very quickly I was back in the shallows and saw that my arm was being held by a woman in a long green dress. My feet touched the bottom and I stood up. I turned to thank the woman but there was no one there. I asked my friends who were racing over to me but they said that there hadn't been anyone else there. They saw me come to the surface on my own. I now believe that it was my guardian angel. She saved me from drowning that day.

Sally, 33

My husband was married before. His wife left him with a young girl, Tania, and ran away with another man. I was already friends with him, but it took quite a long time from the moment when they split up to when we started getting involved. For the first year he was devastated, and it was only as our friendship developed that we started to fall in love with each other.

It took a few months after that before he asked me to move in with him. I was quite nervous about it. It took me a few weeks to say yes. I needed to be absolutely sure he meant it. And I was scared about the idea of trying to take the place of Tania's mother. Up to that point she only knew me as a close friend of her daddy and now that was going to change. She was only six years old and I didn't know what it would be like at all.

The first few days were traumatic. Tania wasn't unpleasant to me, she was just very distant. And I felt so awkward trying to make friends with her, but also trying to make it clear I didn't think I was her "new mummy". I just wanted to be able to look after her without upsetting her. She is a lovely little thing, very sweet and a credit to her dad, and it was distressing that she seemed to be closed off from me.

Gradually, she became a bit less distant and started to tell me a little bit about what she had been doing at school. I knew I just had to be patient and not push things.

I remember the moment when things started to change very clearly. It was late one night and she was supposed to be in bed. I was watching television in my pyjamas, a stupid reality show. I can't remember where my husband was, but I think he must have been working late.

Tania came in and instead of sitting on the other side of the room, she came and cuddled in next to me. I put my arm around her.

I asked her if she missed her mummy. I didn't know if it was the right thing to say but I was worried about her. She said she did and told me she cried sometimes in the night. That made me cry, but I gave her a big hug and told her that I knew I wasn't her mummy but that I would do my best to look after her and be her friend.

She gave me a big hug back and told me I was nice, too, then just settled in to watch the telly. I don't think she even noticed how much I was crying.

I looked up and I saw a faint vision of a woman sitting in the other chair watching us. She was smiling. There was a very faint flicker of light around, and she was only just visible. I felt like she could see right into my soul and knew what I was thinking.

Then I looked back at Tania. She was wrapped up in whatever was going on in the television show. But she curled up against me and we sat there like that together. For the first time I realised a little bit of what it means to be a mother. At that moment I'd have done anything in the world to protect that little girl and to make things happy for her.

I've always done my best to be as good a stepmother to her as I can since then. And now she has a younger stepsister and she has been absolutely brilliant at helping me look after her, too. But I don't think I will ever forget how vulnerable she seemed that night and the way that angel looked at me.

Carly, 28

I nearly lost my little girl at a fairground when she was five. We were standing watching people going round on the carousel. One minute she was there and then the next time I looked around she was gone. There was a big crowd around me and for a few moments I thought she must be close. I started calling her name, getting more and more worried but she didn't turn up.

I'd been worried about losing her in the crowd and I had told her to go the big tent if she did get lost, so the first thing I did was run over there. But there was no sign. Then

I started really panicking. No one seemed to be able to tell me who I could talk to about a lost child. It's so chaotic at those places and no one seemed to be in charge.

I started just running about like a headless chicken, desperately hoping I'd either find her or someone who could help. Then, when I was standing by this big haunted house ride someone tapped me on the shoulder. It was a woman about my age with a kind face and she was holding my daughter's hand. She said something like I think I've got someone that you've lost. I dropped on to my knees and gave my daughter a huge hug. Then I looked up to thank the woman, but she wasn't there. I felt bad about that because I really should have thanked her properly.

Things got strange when I started talking to my daughter about what had happened and how she had got lost. You know how hard it is to get a proper story out of a child that age? Well she gave me a very clear account and it was like this.

When we were by the carousel, she had turned away to look at some toys on a stand and then when she looked back for me there was a man there. He took her hand and told her that I had told him to look after me. He then started leading her quickly away towards the edge of the fair.

I got her to tell me that part a few times as you can imagine. Since I hadn't talked to anyone, it sounds a lot like he was trying to abduct her. I was terrified by that part of the story.

Anyway, then the man had been confronted by the woman I met. She had stood in his way and told him that she was looking after me. He had tried to push past her but my daughter said she got very cross when he did that and gave him a big push. She also shouted something my daughter didn't understand, and the man ran away.

After that the woman led her back to me.

I told my daughter how happy I was that the man hadn't taken her away from me and tried to tell her that she had to be careful about men like that. Also I said how much I wished I could thank the woman who had brought her back to me because I didn't know who she was.

She told me not to be silly. She said the woman was with us a lot. I asked her to repeat that and she said she was often there in the car or in the supermarket as we did the shopping. She said that the woman sometimes pulled funny faces at her when I wasn't looking.

You can imagine the hairs stood up on the back of my neck when I heard that. I certainly had never seen the woman in my life but my daughter just assumed that I was being silly and I must know her.

I asked my daughter to tell me if she ever saw her again, but she never did. But I liked to think that she might be there anyway, smiling at my daughter behind my back when my attention was distracted.

Petra, 34

One day last year I got a sudden feeling that I should call my mother. In fact, it was more than a feeling. I felt like there was a voice in my head that kept telling me to call her.

I had had an argument with her the week before. We'd both said some hurtful things and I really didn't want to be the first one to apologise. So, in every way I didn't want to talk to her. I do love my mother but we have our good weeks and bad weeks and this was during one of the bad weeks.

I couldn't ignore this voice in my head, though, so after about half an hour I gave in. I even remember saying, "Fine, I'll call her, just stop bothering me," as though I was talking to someone. That really sticks in my head given what happened afterwards.

I called her and there was no reply. I tried three times over half an hour because it wasn't a time of day when she would usually be out of the house. Then, because I was getting a strange feeling I called her neighbour Anne, who she is good friends with. I asked if she had seen her and she ended up offering to go round and check, and to leave a message that I had called. (Unbelievably, my mother had still been refusing to buy an answerphone).

When Anne went round she heard my mother inside. She was calling for help. Anne had spare keys so she ran home and let herself in and ran upstairs. My mother had had an accident and was lying on the floor with her ankle twisted sideways, clearly broken. She was in a lot of pain, but extremely relieved to see her neighbour – apparently she had been trying to shout for help for a couple of hours.

What had happened was this: my mother had decided to get a box of clothes down from the attic. This involves climbing up a loft ladder. The ladder is in two sections which are supposed to be held together by a kind of bolt that slides into a hole and secures them together. However as my mother was on the top half of the ladder, the catch had failed and the whole thing had collapsed under her weight.

It is not a great distance to fall, but one of her legs had got caught between the ladder and the floor as she landed and she had a badly broken ankle.

She had lain there in shock for some time, before realising that she wasn't going to be able to reach the phone. She could barely drag herself across the floor of the landing, let alone get down the stairs. So she had decided she had to shout for help, but the house is far enough back from the road that no-one had heard, not even the neighbours. She admitted that she was getting hysterical with fear by the time she heard Anne at the door. And who can blame her, given the terrible pain she must have been in. She lives alone, so couldn't be absolutely sure that anyone would come round and she was having to con-template the idea of getting down the stairs even with her ankle in that condition.

So it was incredibly fortunate that I decided to call when I did. But I don't really believe in luck. I think somehow I got a message that my mother needed me. As I said, I had no intention of calling her that week until I suddenly felt that urge to call her immediately, and even then I couldn't rest until I had talked to Anne and left a message, and that was the reason why she went round when she did.

My mother's leg is better now. I try to call her more often, even when we are not getting on so well – and we have finally persuaded her to get not only an answerphone, but also a mobile phone!

Kayleigh, 22

I think I was helped by an angel on my first day in a new job last year.

I had been out of work for about five months and had lost a lot of confidence when I was offered a great job at a local newspaper. I was very nervous about it in advance and was having anxiety attacks the week before, but I knew this was an important opportunity as it was a chance to put my qualifications to work.

The first morning was utterly horrendous. I was sharing an office with two girls who seemed to absolutely despise me. They wouldn't help me work out the tiniest thing. If I asked where the photocopier was they would just vaguely gesture and expect me to find it myself. They virtually refused to talk to me, and if I came back into the office they would suddenly stop talking as though they had been saying something nasty about me.

It was awful and I had no idea what I had done to deserve to be treated in this way. It got to the point where just before my lunch break I panicked and decided to run away. I walked out of the main door and more or less ran down the street to the nearest park.

I sat there and cried for a good ten minutes, letting out all the frustrations and upset of the morning. Then I sat feeling bleak and hopeless because I was losing this one chance to make my life better.

That was when a lady came and sat down beside me. She asked me what was wrong and I told her a bit of what I was going through. She was lovely, very sympathetic. She told me that all workplaces had difficult people in them but that I would get through it. And she also told me that if they were being mean to me, they were the ones who had a problem, not me.

It was powerful advice, but I felt like it was too late. I had run away and now had tear streaks all over my face. She led me to the public toilets in the park and helped me wash my face, then pointed out that for all anyone knew I had simply popped out for some early lunch. She was right, it wasn't irrevocable.

I pulled myself together, thanked the lady and marched back to work. In the afternoon the two girls were still very difficult but I remembered what the lady had said about it being their problem and managed to ignore them.

The next day was much better. The man who was my supervisor had been in meetings all day on the day before, but now he spent some time with me talking through what I needed to know. And he introduced me to some other people round the building, some of whom seemed really nice. I started to feel less isolated, and to understand what I was doing, and because I was concentrating hard and not worrying, I stopped noticing the two girls in my office.

Then at the start of the following week, there was a reorganisation and I ended up sitting out in the open plan area where I was much happier and started to feel part of the crowd. It would have been terrible if I had given up that easily because I love this job and have ended up with some great friends here. The two girls who were being unpleasant that first week are now gone anyway, so I'm glad I didn't let them get to me.

The interesting thing that I haven't mentioned is that I recognised the lady who talked to me. When I was a kid I used to see this lady watching me when I was playing outside. She would be standing across the road, or looking out of a window, and I came to know her face well. When I was a kid I didn't question why this lady was there looking out for me. Once when I fell out of a tree (only from the lower branches), she helped pick me up, brushed me down and reassured me that the cut on my knee wasn't that bad.

She wasn't a friend of my parents so far as I know and I never saw her when I was with other people. And now that I am grown up and living in a city a long way from my village, it seems most peculiar that she should suddenly be there again in one of my most stressful moments.

I don't know who she is, whether she is some kind of spiritual guide or angel in my life, or just someone who acted very kindly at that moment. But I know she has been there for me before and I hope that if I ever have difficult times in the future she might be there for me again.

Helen, 20

I had this experience one night three years ago when I was finding it difficult to fall asleep. I looked up to see what time it was because I had to get up early for an important job interview.

At the same time I saw a movement from the corner of my eye and when I turned to look, an angel was emerging through the wardrobe doors. I stared at it for a while and then I must have fallen asleep. When I woke up I felt really refreshed and the job interview went very well. And I got the job.

A few weeks later I woke up and the angel was there again. He had a little boy with him and I recognised my baby brother who had died when he was twelve months old. I reached out to the little boy but when I did both he and the angel disappeared.

The next day I was going swimming with my friends. We were diving in the deep end of the pool when my swimsuit got caught on one of the filters near the bottom of the pool. I struggled to get free and I could feel myself choking on the water.

I was losing strength and was certain that I was going to drown. Suddenly, I heard a voice saying, "Stop struggling." I stopped and as soon as I did I felt my swimsuit break free and I floated to the surface.

The pool guards hadn't noticed me struggling and my friends were just having fun and didn't realise what was happening because the pool was quite busy. I think it was my guardian angel visiting me the night before and saved my life at the pool.

Tomas, 38

Alcoholism creeps up on you. I was married with two young children. I always liked a drink, and my wife and I would often have a glass of wine with dinner, as well as enjoying going out to a bar when we had a babysitter.

However, looking back I can see that things slowly changed. We went out less as we were in a period when money was tight. In addition, I was going through a stressful time at work. Increasingly, I would come home from work and, instead of drinking a beer or two in a sociable way, I would drink to get drunk. I would have gin or wine if need be, but often I would just drink enough beer to make sure I was drunk enough to sleep.

It got to the point where I couldn't really sleep if I hadn't had enough alcohol. I would start sweating and twitching and having weird dreams. And then that seemed like a good enough reason to drink more the next night.

After a certain point, I got so bad that I was always snoring in bed at night. After a few nights of waking up and finding my wife sleeping on the sofa in the living room, I started offering to sleep there so I wouldn't keep her awake.

This seemed reasonable to me, even though she looked a bit sad about it. Of course, what I didn't think about was the possibility that instead of not drinking, I might make the choice to not drink and sleep in the bedroom. Clearly the alcohol was becoming more important to me than my relationships.

I was what is known as a "functioning alcoholic". I didn't do anything terrible or embarrassing. Sometimes my wife and I would argue while we were drunk. Sometimes I would fall off the sofa in the night. But I wasn't a complete disaster and that made me feel that I wasn't really an alcoholic, just someone who was going through a stressful time and drinking a little too much.

To give you one more example of the gradual way this creeps up on you, I used to go to the shop and try to decide how much alcohol to buy. My wife drank wine or nothing, so I never needed to make a decision for her. But for myself I would often buy twelve cans of beer. I would justify this to myself on the basis that there was a special offer where six cans cost the same as four, so it was sensible to stock up and I wasn't really going to drink it all.

And then once I had drunk the first six cans I would inevitably move on to drinking all the rest. By that time I was drunk and incapable of making the right decision.

The turning point came one night when even the twelve cans weren't enough for me. I told my wife I was walking to the shop to buy some more. She just looked very sad, but at that exact moment I didn't care. She had got the children to bed and was reading a book herself. I had got to the point where I didn't think she really cared about me any more.

So I went outside and then it seemed like a long way to the shop, so I decided to take the car. Again, this is a stupid thing to do and I am embarrassed to tell you, but I feel I need to be honest in order to explain the situation.

I drove out from our drive, and on down the road. To start with I felt incredibly happy, because it seemed like such fun to be driving the car while I was drunk. Then, inevitably, I lost control, and skidded off the road. I was extremely lucky because all that happened was that I skidded down a slight slope into a field.

I could have killed someone, I could have wrecked the car or hurt myself, so I am not proud at all of that stupid moment. But I just found myself sitting in the car on the edge of that field, with my headlights stretching out into the nothingness of the darkness. The car came close to rolling over but in the end it just lifted up on one side and fell back down in the mud.

At that moment I realised that there was someone in the car with me. You might think I imagined this, since I had been drinking. But I have a very clear memory of it and whether it was in my head or real, it had a huge impact on me.

There was a man sitting in the back seat. He said, "Well, this is a mess, isn't it?" I said, "The car is fine, I'm fine, what's the problem?"

He just looked at me in the rear view mirror. His eyes were terrible, but kind. I knew they were the eyes of an angel.

As I looked into those eyes I saw my wife and children. I imagined them at my funeral, and that made me feel terrible. But then, even worse, I thought about my wife, at home, feeling like I didn't care about her. I remembered all the times my children had come to talk to me and I had been a bit drunk and hadn't wanted to talk to them. I thought about the childhood memories I was creating for them. The drunken father who sometimes ended the evening shouting at his wife, and sometimes snoring drunkenly on the sofa.

I felt humiliated and ridiculous. I looked at myself sitting there in that car in the field, and thought about how I could have died just out of the stupid need to have another beer.

I looked again in the mirror and the man was still there. He tapped himself on the head in a symbol I knew from my father, meaning "think about it".

Then I blinked and he was gone.

I got out of the car and walked straight home. I went to my wife and told her what had happened. Not about the angel. I felt shy and weird about that.

But I told her how stupid I had been to get in the car and how I had crashed, or gone off the road. And I told her how I had realised that the most important things in my life were her and the children, and that I didn't know how I could have been so stupid as to be such a drunkard.

Of course I was still quite drunk at this moment, so although she gave me a big hug and a kiss, I still went and slept on the sofa. I hardly slept a wink though and as soon as I heard her moving in the morning I went and told her everything again. To start with she was sceptical, she pointed out I had said all the same things last night. I think she thought I had forgotten.

I told her though that I knew that. I just wanted to tell her again now so she would believe me. I promised to reform my ways. I vowed to give up drink for a month to prove I was serious.

From that moment I worked hard at being a better husband and father. I worked with the children on their homework, I read books to them and played the piano for them while they practised their instruments (one plays violin, the other the flute). I stayed sober so I could talk to my wife. I think I fell in love with her all over again, to be honest.

I got to the end of that month and I realised I didn't want to drink any more. It had been tough in the first week or so to not drink, but now my body had adjusted and I could see how much better my life was without alcohol.

Ten years later, I am so happy that I managed to turn my life around that corner. Today I will have the occasional glass of beer on a Saturday or a champagne at a wedding. But no more. Alcohol no longer rules my life.

I think it is the most insidious drug in some ways because it is legal and quite acceptable, so when you are sliding into dependency no one notices or warns you until it is too late. In my case it took a moment of great foolishness and a warning from an angel to make me realise exactly how it was wrecking my life.

Tom, 79

I was evacuated from London in the early days of the war. We lived in Stepney, which was bombed a great deal because it is near the river and the docks.

I was eight years old. I remember being at the station, holding my gas mask and my toy tiger – we were only allowed one toy. I was wearing an overcoat that was a bit too big for me – it had originally belonged to my elder brother Robert, who had enlisted in the army. My mum thought I should take it as it would have "room to grow".

I was devastated at being sent away from my mum. I thought she would forget me, or that she would be killed and I would never see her again. I couldn't understand why she couldn't come with me.

At the station she seemed very calm, while I was on the verge of tears. Looking back now I know she wasn't calm at all, but was trying to put on a brave face so I wouldn't be upset. She wanted me to think of it as though it was a long holiday and kept telling me to be good for whoever chose me to live with them.

One of the saddest moments of my life was when I looked out of the train window and saw my mother waving goodbye to me.

I ended up in a village in Kent. It's only about fifty miles from Stepney – these days you'd drive down there in less than an hour. But it seemed like a different country. I'd never been to the countryside before and I remember being amazed by all the greenery and the smells and noises.

I was taken in by the Green family, who ran a small farm. They were really good people. They could be a bit quiet and distant, but over time I came to know them well and I ended up going back to see them many times after the war.

I wouldn't say it was like a holiday, but it was an interesting experience in many ways. I discovered a love for the countryside that is still with me – I live down in Devon now. I was able to roam the fields and hedgerows and learn all about how a farm works.

I missed my mother terribly and constantly worried about her. I would get a letter from her every Monday and on the few occasions it came a day late I went round in a fog of fear thinking she must have been caught up in a bombing raid.

I was there for five years in the end. My mother came and visited a few times, though it was hard for her because the train fares weren't cheap and money was tight. The Greens came to feel like my second family, but my heart always stayed with my family. My elder brother Robert died in North Africa in 1941. He was still only a child himself really, just nineteen years old. Thankfully my mother survived and we were happily reunited. If my evacuation had been the saddest day, the day the war was finally over was one of the happiest days of my life. The whole of London was out on the streets. It was like the best party you've ever been to, only better.

After the war my mother told me that she had seen an angel the day we set off for the countryside. While she was standing on the platform, holding back the tears she didn't want me to see, she had felt a hand on her shoulder. This was as the train was just about to set off. She had looked back momentarily and seen a kind woman, with lovely eyes. Then the train started and she started frantically waving at me through the window, and at that moment she saw the same woman standing behind me inside the train, with her hand on my shoulder. She understood this to mean that there was an angel watching over me.

I don't remember any of this, but in the chaos it is not surprising. But really in the end I know I should count my blessings. We lost my brother, but we made it through those terrible times to the better life that lay beyond the war.

Helping Hands

Sometimes in life we need a little bit of help, not only in emergencies, but in the ordinary trials and tribulations of everyday life. If we are lucky, we will have family or friends who can give us a helping hand, or perhaps workmates or neighbours. In other situations it may be a stranger who comes to our aid. And sometimes, that stranger might just be an angel who has taken pity on us or chosen to show us some kindness.

Cody, 53

One time I was on a long drive, taking some furniture from Oregon to Denver. I stopped at a gas station miles from anywhere. This young man came over to me. He was dressed in ragged clothes and looked unshaven and a bit unwashed. My first instinct was to get in the car and lock the door, but he started to talk to me and he seemed normal enough.

He told me that he had had his wallet stolen and also that his car was a few miles down the road as he had run out of gas. He had walked to this place in the hope of persuading the owner to let him have some gas on credit but he had been turned away. He seemed genuine and also I trusted him. So even though it might have seemed a risky thing to do, I bought a can full of petrol for him then offered him a lift to his car.

This is the point when, if he had been a conman or thief, I could have got into trouble. Afterwards, my wife told me off for being so trusting, but sometimes you just have to help people rather than treating them all as criminals.

I took him to his car and gave him my address in Denver, not really expecting to get my money back.

As I drove away I looked sideways and just for a second I saw a striking blonde woman smiling at me, and thanking me. Then I blinked and she wasn't there any more. It was an odd moment, not like anything that has ever happened to me before. I felt that an angel had seen me taking a risk and helping someone out and had felt moved to let me know I'd done the right thing.

Two weeks later I got a letter in the post. It was from the young man. He sent two ten-dollar bills to cover my expenses. He also sent me a photograph of a new born boy – he had just become an uncle for the first time and he wanted me to know that without my help he wouldn't have made it back in time to help his sister to the hospital.

I've still got the letter, partly because of one thing he wrote in it. He said, "When this little one grows up I hope he doesn't get into any trouble. But if he ever does I only hope he finds a passing angel like you who can help him out."

Of course, I'm not an angel, but I still think of that woman I saw that day and believe that she probably was.

Nora, 39

I am a home-care nurse and much of my job is looking after terminal patients who won't get better. My job is to regulate their medication, make sure they're comfortable and support their families.

I had one patient about two years ago, a ninety-year-old man who was dying of cancer and he and his wife wanted him to die at home. I had the night shift looking after the man. I would sit by his bed and make sure he was as comfortable as possible.

One night as I sat by his bed I saw a strange reflection in

the window. It was dark outside but I could see a shape standing outside looking in. I was very tired and decided that I hadn't seen anything. I turned my attention back to my patient. Suddenly I saw the shape in the window again. This time I went to the window to investigate. I looked out onto the garden but it was empty and silent. When I turned around I saw something that amazed me. There was a woman standing by the bed, cradling the man's head in her hands. As I watched she slowly faded away. When I went back to my patient he had died.

I went upstairs to tell his wife and I had an urge to tell her what I'd seen. She told me that she was grateful for me telling her. She had been asking the angels to come for him because she couldn't bear to see him suffering.

Selma, 42

Last week my daughter had her school concert. I had to go to a work meeting first and stupidly I lost my way on the way back. The meeting had over-run and I was short of time as it was. I don't have a sat-nav and I didn't have a map. I left the motorway because there was a really bad traffic jam and I thought I'd be able to find my way back, but I just ended up driving round and round these villages and getting lost in industrial estates.

I really didn't want to miss her concert. My ex-husband missed a lot of these kinds of things when he was looking after her, and she had been upset by it, so I had solemnly promised I would be there. And now time was running away from me as I drove up and down these stupid country lanes trying to find my way back to the main road.

Twice I asked people the way and then got lost again trying to follow their directions. I don't know if they explained it badly or if I was just in such a panic I couldn't remember what they had said five minutes down the road.

Eventually I just pulled up at the side of the road and put my head in my hands. I couldn't even phone the school to warn her, because my mobile had run out of power. I was feeling like a terrible parent, like I shouldn't have arranged this meeting in the first place because I should have known things would go wrong.

Then, though the windows were closed, I felt this warm, scented wind in the car. I felt a kind of peace and calm come into the car, and for some reason decided to give it one last go. I decided I would just go with my instinct and see what happened.

It was like driving on autopilot after that. Every time I came to a junction, I knew as I was approaching it which way I was going to turn. I didn't even bother trying to read the signposts, I just trusted the instincts and kept driving. And then, finally I found my way back to the main road. It was only about five miles from the point where I had left it in the first place, but ironically the traffic jam had totally cleared while I was messing about on the back roads.

I pulled up outside the school with about a minute to spare, feeling incredibly lucky and blessed to have managed to get there at all. As I turned to get out of the car

Helping Hands

I saw something unexpected on the back seat. It was three white feathers, very bright against the brown of the seats.

I picked up those feathers and held them tightly in my hand all the way through my daughter's performance, and I gave thanks to whoever or whatever had come into my car and helped me find my way.

Ben, 25

About ten years ago when we were about fifteen years old, my best friend and I ran away from home. My house was very small and always overcrowded and I had to share a bedroom with my two younger brothers who went to bed earlier than me and the kitchen/living room was always occupied by my parents and often their friends. My friend Ross had problems with his father who was a violent alcoholic.

We didn't really know where to go so we took the bus to the next city north of the one where we grew up and when we got there we just hung around the mall because we didn't know what else to do. We were very young. The money we took with us only lasted just over a week and we inevitably got very hungry. We tried to get jobs but everywhere we asked told us that we didn't look old enough and they wanted to see some ID to prove our ages, so it was all beginning to seem hopeless.

We went to stand near a hotdog stall and decided to try to trick the man working there to give us some hotdogs.

We would ask and pretend we had money and then when we got the food we'd run. We both asked for hotdogs with all the trimmings and then tried to run but the man was ready for us and chased after us.

He was going to call the police but a little girl came up to us and gave us $10.00. She told us it was for our food and we gave some of it to the stallholder so he wouldn't call the police on us. The little girl went off to where a couple was waiting for her. We presumed that they must be her parents. Her mother looked at us and said, "It's time to go home, boys." We looked at each other, thinking how did she know? When we looked back the family had vanished. They were nowhere in sight.

We talked for a while and decided to go home. The money that the little girl had given us was enough to buy bus tickets back to our city and we decided to go to my house first and face the music. I thought my parents would be furious but they were just really glad to see us and relieved that we were safe.

Everybody had been looking for us and my dad told us that Ross's parents had split up after his mom had kicked his father out so he could go home and it would be a peaceful place now. It also meant that we could hang out at his house when my younger brothers went to bed. We still don't know how the family who helped us knew about our situation or how they just disappeared but they helped us in so many ways. To us they were a family of angels.

Jenny, 34

My best friend's husband left her last year and, seeing as she worked nights, I agreed to look after her children while she went to work until she could make other arrangements. I have a daughter who was nine months old at the time so I used to take her with me. It was a fairly long drive, at least an hour there and back but my friend was in such a state that I knew I had to help her. By the end of the week I was exhausted and the drive home seemed interminable. I was yawning and I could feel my eyes starting to close. I did think about pulling over but I just wanted to get home and go to bed.

I remember driving on a winding road around the mountains but then my eyes must have closed because I heard a car honking its horn. I glanced to my left and saw a car with a man driving it. He moved his lips and seemed to be saying, "Wake up." When I glanced to the left again, however, there was no car in sight. The road lane was empty even though I had a good view up ahead.

I have often wondered if the man driving that car was an angel sent to warn me. If he hadn't woken me up I would have driven off the road and possibly both my daughter and I could have been killed.

Katie, 48

When I was a student in the 1980s I had a job as a receptionist in a hairdressers to earn a bit of extra money. My university was on campus outside the town so I had a car to help me get around. The salon didn't close until 9.00 pm on a Thursday so that everyone could come in after work and get their hair done for the weekend.

I remember one particularly cold Thursday night when it had started to snow. All the clients had gone home and I was clearing up for the night. As I turned off the lights at the back of the salon where the coffee machine is, I heard the door open and when I went back into the salon I saw that an elderly man had come inside. I told him that we were closed and that all the hairstylists had left.

He seemed disappointed but then asked me if he could sit for a few moments to dry out. It was when he said that that I noticed that his clothes were completely dry. I was quite anxious to get back to the college but I told him that he could stay for a short while and I offered him a cup of coffee. I made one for myself as well as him and we sat and chatted for a while, mainly about my studies. He was a really nice man and I actually had a nice time talking to him.

Eventually he said he had to go and left the salon, and said, "Thank you, Katie," which was odd because I was sure that I didn't tell him my name. Because I was in a hurry I thought no more about it and I finished turning the lights out, locked the door and looked for the man because

I was going to offer him a lift in my car. I couldn't see him and the pavements were empty in both directions. I thought that maybe someone else had offered him a lift and got in my car to drive home.

About half a mile down the road, there were flashing police lights and several ambulances. There had been a really bad accident with several fatalities. If the elderly man hadn't made me wait a while before leaving I may have been involved in the crash. He saved me.

Nell, 55

Many years ago when my children were still very young, I had to work late and my parents had the children while I worked. My husband had left me two months earlier so it was a difficult time for me. When my husband took our family car I only had enough money to buy an ancient Ford with a broken fuel gauge. I had to check the miles on the clock and estimate in my head how much petrol there would be left in it.

One night the car began coughing as I drove home. I'd forgotten to check the mileage and the car had run out of petrol. I pulled over to the side of the road and looked to see if there were any cars coming up who could perhaps give me a lift to the nearest garage to get some fuel. It was an empty moorland road and I could see nobody.

I was panicking because this was before mobile phones and I had no way of contacting anyone. It was a few miles to the nearest village and I didn't fancy walking alone in the dark. I closed my eyes and said a silent prayer for someone to come and help me out. When I opened my eyes there was a man staring at me through the driver's side window.

I wasn't scared because there was something about the way he looked. He seemed so calm and kind that the voice in my head told me to trust him and I rolled down the window. He was smartly dressed and smelled of washing powder. He suggested pushing the car over the hill so that I could then roll down the hill into the village.

The man told me to put the car in neutral and he made his way to the back of the car. I carefully steered the car around the bend and eventually we reached the top of the hill. I turned round to thank the man but he had vanished. I looked up and down the road but as far as I looked I couldn't see anyone.

I got back in the car, took off the handbrake and I rolled down the hill into the village. I will never forget that experience and even today as I head towards old age I know it was an angel who helped me.

Sarah, 39

Back in 2002, I was driving home with my three daughters in the car. They had been doing a concert at their school and it was now quite late in the evening and dark and cold. There wasn't a lot of traffic but suddenly a man sprinted across the road. He was dressed all in black and looked to be very tall. I was so startled that I cried out and braked sharply so as not to hit him. At that very second a flatbed truck came racing out of a side road. If I hadn't braked for the man dressed in black it would have hit me side on and could have injured or killed my little girls.

I was stunned for a few moments. Then I got out of the car to make sure that the man I nearly hit was OK. I looked around but he had completely vanished. It was as if he ran across in front of me to make me brake so that the truck wouldn't hit me. Was he an angel? I think he could have been.

Finlay, 18

When my mum found out that she was pregnant with me my dad took on extra work at a building firm to save up for the baby. He worked weekends on urgent jobs to get the overtime pay.

One Sunday when he was clearing rubble from the site of a demolished factory he heard a voice telling him to stop. He looked around from his bulldozer but there was no one nearby then he heard the voice again say "Stop!"

He got out of his bulldozer and looked around. Beneath the rubble in front of him he saw something metal with a dull sheen. He suddenly realised what it was. It was an unexploded World War II bomb.

He immediately phoned the police and they came out and confirmed his suspicions and cordoned off the area. The bomb was safely detonated with a controlled explosion. My dad told my mum that it must have been his guardian angel telling him to stop clearing the area. The bomb could have detonated and killed him if he had tried to move it with a bulldozer.

Tara, 43

I don't want to be too specific, but in the 1980s I volunteered at a refugee camp helping with the victims of a famine in Africa. It was an upsetting experience for me, but at the same time I knew that any distress I was feeling was completely worthless compared to the suffering of the people we were trying to help. They had escaped from militias who were fighting for territory. Many of them had lost family and friends and were traumatised. It was all we could do to try and keep them alive.

I'm not sure if I would say it was a good experience. I still wake up sometimes having nightmares about it. But on the other hand it taught me some huge lessons. I know that any fatuous problems I may be going through in my personal life are nothing against the things those people went through.

It was a huge camp, with tents in long lines stretching out across this barren terrain. We had to try and provide twice daily meals and the refugees waited in these long hopeless lines as we shared out the limited, bland supplies we had.

There was an area where we stayed as volunteers and I spent a lot of time there. But sometimes I would go and walk around the camp. The main thing I remember is the way that the people there seemed so resigned to their situations. There were babies born there and while we tried to celebrate their births it was impossible to hide the feeling that this was the worst possible start to life. And no one knew how long the camp would be there for.

One night I walked on my own all the way through the camp to the perimeter. There was a military presence at the fence because there was a slight danger that the fighting would reach the camp. I went up to the wire fence that bounded the camp and looked out across the scrubland and I saw an angel standing there. She was looking at the camp with an expression of terrible sadness. I would say that there was a look of anger there, too. And who can be surprised by that when us humans treat each other with such contempt and abuse?

Sandra, 48

A few years ago, my husband and I moved to a small farm. We had sold our place in the city and given up our jobs to find a more peaceful way of life in the country. My husband's grandfather gave us a cow as a "farm-warming" present. He also taught me to milk her by hand. I called her Blossom and grew to be very fond of her and I spent much of that summer going for walks with her around the fields.

Later that year on the day when the first snow had fallen, I felt someone pull me out of sleep by tugging on my arms. I woke up and couldn't see anything there but felt a bit strange so I got up for a drink of water. I kept looking out towards the barn and for some reason felt compelled to put my boots on and go and investigate.

When I opened the barn door I could see Blossom lying on the floor as if she was in pain. I immediately went over to help her and somehow got her to her feet. At her feet something was wet and wriggling and when I bent down to look I saw that she had given birth. The calf was a boy who then got to his feet as mum gave him a good lick. As I watched, he began suckling.

I felt that something had woken me deliberately because Blossom needed me. An angel was looking out for me and my pet.

Healing Angels

Sometimes we need healing or medical assistance when our life is in danger. But there are also many less dramatic times in our life when we need other kinds of healing. In some of these accounts we hear from people who believe that angels have been able to help them overcome or recover from ailments and injuries of a variety of sorts, from pneumonia to a broken heart. In other cases we hear of angels giving succour and comfort to those whose illness is beyond assistance.

Tomas, 25

I used to suffer from terrible migraines. They made it impossible for me to do anything except lie in a darkened room with a towel over my face.

People don't really understand migraines. They are not just bad headaches. They are far more of a problem. You get these kinds of blinding lights coming out of the corners of your eyes, you feel nauseous. Sounds is unbearable, and you lose a sense of balance. In short everything around you causes you pain and it is very hard to deal with even basic tasks as long as the migraine lasts. I found painkillers didn't really work – they dulled the edge of the migraine, but they didn't take it away completely and I was still incapacitated.

The only thing that used to help me when I was in the grip of a terrible migraine was knowing that there was an angel looking after me. She was a tall, elegant woman who was usually wearing a blue dress. I would feel her hand on my forehead as I lay there in the dark room. Sometimes I saw her standing behind me.

She used to talk to me now and then, telling me that the pain was only temporary and that I could make it through it. She also told me that if I felt a migraine coming I should think of her.

After that, at the first sign of a migraine, the first time I felt those twinges and the feeling of light in the corners of my eyes being uncomfortable, I used to go and sit down for a few moments and think about her. Sometimes in those moments I felt her hand on the top of my head, feeling warm and soothing. Other times I just thought about her face and her calm presence and how she had helped me.

Gradually, I started to be able to conquer the migraines. It didn't happen overnight, sometimes I still got them whatever I did. But, little by little, I managed to make them go away. I would feel the first signs, go somewhere quiet and think of my angel and gradually that warm feeling would spread from the top of my head down through my head and neck and I would start to relax and then I would realise that the symptoms were fading.

I haven't had a migraine for over a year now. But I still know that if I feel one coming on, I may be able to make it go away by concentrating on my angel.

Celia, 35

I had pneumonia while I was living in Hong Kong. I blame that humid heat they have in the summer. I got a chest infection and it just kept getting worse until I was wheezing. I delayed going to the hospital because I wasn't sure whether my health insurance covered it and I was trying to keep working and then finally I ended up collapsing and having to be taken to hospital as an emergency patient.

When I woke up the first time I saw an angel standing at the bottom of the bed. She was looking worried, but told me to rest, so I went back to sleep. Then the next time I woke up the doctor was there and my flatmate. I was in a pretty bad state, having trouble breathing and on heavy medication.

For a few days I was very ill. I often saw the angel at the end of my bed when no one else was there. No one believes me about this but I know what I saw and I was not dreaming. She started to smile a little on the second day. She didn't talk to me much, she just used to watch over me and occasionally she came and stroked my forehead.

I was out of danger after a few days. I told my flatmate what I had seen and she just laughed at me. But it made me see things in a different way. I had never believed in a spiritual realm before that, but now I believe that there are angels out there and perhaps other spirits that we cannot even comprehend.

Jacqueline, 53

I am a nurse. I see people who are sick and dying regularly and there aren't always angels there for them. There can't be. God or the angels simply can't help every suffering soul that passes through the hospital. But I have seen angels on a few occasions.

Once there was a girl who was in the hospital after a serious house fire. She was in a room on her own with major burns and the nurses on that ward were having to look after her fairly constantly. The room had a glass window looking on to the nurses' area.

Gradually her burns started to heal. I was down there one day talking to one of my friends on the ward and she told me to look through the window. She asked if I could see someone in there. I looked hard and saw nothing. She just gave me a strange look and changed the subject.

I was fascinated by this and started to find excuses to wander past the girl's room. Two nights later I did see someone in there. It was an attractive woman wearing a cream dress and some pearls. She had lovely blonde hair that hung down loose to her shoulders.

She was just standing there at the end of the bed watching the girl. I walked on down the corridor, and when I came back a moment or two later she wasn't there.

This whole event was a little surprising as this was the middle of the night. There were not supposed to be any visitors in the ward.

I checked with reception and they said no one had been in or out. I told my friend about it a couple of days later and she was relieved I'd seen her, too. She told me that she had seen her several times and no one would believe her so she had stopped trying to persuade anyone that there was an angel in there watching over the girl.

The other time I saw an angel was far more traumatic. A young teenage boy came in from the emergency room. He had been stabbed and had lost a lot of blood before they could get him in for treatment.

He was on a trolley being pushed into surgery and as well as the doctors and nurses who were there trying to keep him alive for long enough for the surgeons to operate, there was a tall, noble-looking man walking behind the trolley. My attention was drawn to him because he looked so sad, and also because no one else seemed to be seeing him. He just drifted along behind the trolley in this very solemn way as all the others bustled about. No one walked into him, but no one looked straight at him.

When the boy went into theatre, the man stayed outside looking through the doors. He leaned his forehead on the window, and looked devastated as he watched.

I heard later that the boy died. It was such a waste. He was only a kid and it had happened because of some stupid argument over whether he looked at another kid the wrong way or not. The boy who killed him went to prison but for some ridiculously short amount of time. I'm sorry but I don't accept that a kid with a knife is any less responsible for murder than fully grown man with a gun. It is still murder, the taking of someone's life. These kids talk about "respect" a lot. I'd like to see them try to explain that to God, that they killed a boy because he didn't respect them enough.

Anyway, the last I saw of that man was him leaning on the doors of the operating theatre. I am not as sure that he was an angel as the woman I saw with the girl with the burns. But he had the same unworldly air about him and no one seemed to think that the boy had come in with any friends or relatives, so I think he may well have been an angel, too. As I said, the angels can't always save us, and when us humans manage to behave in such stupid, evil ways as stabbing each other for no good reason, it must make the angels weep for us.

Teresa, 23

A few years ago I developed a lot of problems with my health. I got repeated bouts of abdominal pain and spent a lot of time in bed. My doctor told me that it would be best if they removed my appendix but I have always been terrified of having an anaesthetic and surgery.

I told him that I would think about it and went home. I remember praying quietly asking to get better so that I wouldn't need to have my appendix removed.

A couple of days later I had a dream where a woman stood by my bed and gently put her hands on my stomach. She told me not to be afraid and said that she had come to heal me.

I got the most incredible amount of love and kindness from her and I felt very peaceful. Her skin was so pale that it seemed to glow and she was wearing a very long white dress.

When I woke up, I was completely better. From that day forwards I have never had any problems with my appendix and have never needed surgery. My doctor is astonished and says it's a miracle. I didn't tell him about my healing angel but I know that it is down to her.

Gillian, 36

My son, Luke, was diagnosed with bone cancer at just ten years old. Because of his illness, his immune system doesn't work so well. About three months ago he developed an infection and had to go into hospital. I spent as much time with him in the hospital as I could. They even put a spare bed in the room with him so I could stay overnight.

One evening I was sitting quietly by his bedside feeling utterly miserable. I began to pray that he would get better and his suffering would end. A nurse came into the room to check his temperature and I noticed that she had a different uniform on than the rest of the nurses that I'd met. It was a dress and apron instead of the tunics and trousers that all the other nurses wore. She took his temperature and smoothed his brow then smiled at me and said, "Nearly better."

The next day, Luke's infection had cleared up. A month later his cancer was in remission and he needed no further treatment other than a test in five years time. As I said goodbye to the hospital staff who had looked after him so well, I mentioned the nurse I had seen on his last night in hospital. As I described her the nurse gave me a funny look. She told me that no nurses had dressed like that since the 1960s. She must have been an angel come to answer my prayers and make him better.

Helena, 27

A few years ago my mom was in hospital with a severe case of septicaemia. She was in hospital for about two weeks and because her condition was so bad doctors warned us that she might not survive. They told my dad that they had done all they medically could for her.

My dad was in shock. My mom and him had been married for thirty years. We went home and I told Dad to take a sleeping pill and go to bed.

I told him that I'd stay by the phone in case the hospital phoned with bad news. By four in the morning I was very tired and beginning to doze a bit.

Suddenly, I heard a very kind and loving male voice telling me to wake up. The voice told me that Mom was going to be fine and I should go to bed. I woke up instantly and looked around the room but there was no one there. Exhausted I went up to bed just as daylight was beginning to break through.

The next morning, Dad said that he heard me coming up to bed because he had been woken by a voice telling him that his wife would survive.

I told him what had happened to me in the night and we were both amazed. The voice he heard was a gentle male voice, too.

The next morning we went to the hospital and Mom was awake and more aware than she had been since falling ill. She told us that angels had visited her during the night and given her the choice of going with them or staying. She chose to stay and miraculously she got better and resumed her life just as before.

Frederick, 57

I saw an angel when I was in hospital. I was only in for a minor operation on an abscess, but after I came out of the operation I became extremely ill with an infection.

The doctors had me on a drip with painkillers and strong antibiotics, but my fever kept getting worse. I was in a lot of pain but I was also hallucinating, so it is possible that what I saw was an illusion, but it seemed extremely real at the time.

I had fallen asleep for what could have been a few moments or hours later at night. I looked up and the room was empty, but completely full of a bright light. There was an angel standing beside me. He put his palm on my forehead and left it there as though he was taking my temperature.

I tried to talk to him and struggle, but he just put his hand out, with the palm towards me, indicating that I should stay calm.

As his hand stayed on my forehead, I felt my head start to cool slightly and all the confused thoughts that had been whirling round my head started to fade away. Then he took his hand away and left the room.

I fell into the deepest sleep I had had in days, without dreams or nightmares. When I woke up I was still ill, but the fever had broken slightly and the doctors were starting to look less worried when they stopped to check me. I gradually recovered until I was able to leave the hospital a few days later. I was weak for months after that infection, but in the end I got over it.

Kathy, 46

About two years ago I had minor surgery on my back and in the weeks that followed I experienced a lot of severe migraine headaches. I was told that this was a side effect of the surgery and would eventually go away.

I was going through a terrible time, the headaches were stopping me from getting enough sleep and I began to pray that they would stop and I could finally feel some peace. I went to sleep that night feeling that it was a turning point and that things would get better.

Some time during that night I woke up and saw a beautiful creature standing at the foot of my bed. It looked at first like a white shadow and I couldn't make out any features, but then it turned and looked at me and it had such a peaceful, kind face. I wasn't at all afraid because I knew that God had sent this creature to answer my prayers. It slowly glided up to where my head was and then cradled my head in its hands. I could feel myself relaxing in its gentle grip.

The next day I woke up and felt incredible peace and calm. I had no headache that day and when I went to sleep that night I didn't have any difficulty dropping off. I haven't had a headache since.

Gillian, 32

An angel came to me in the form of a white cat when I was trying to recover from a broken heart.

I know I sound a bit melodramatic, but when my boyfriend ran off with my best friend I felt like I had been smashed into pieces. My stepmother took pity on me and lent me this cottage she has down in Devon. It was February so the weather was ghastly. I tried going out for bracing country walks but for the most part I just got soaked and frozen, so I spent a lot of time just sitting staring at the walls, feeling like I was losing my mind.

I kept going over all the little details of how it had happened and how I hadn't noticed. The times I'd left them together, how pleased I'd been that they had got on so well together. And how absolutely traumatised I'd been when I caught them in bed together. I'd expected them to tell me it was a stupid mistake, but it turned out it had been going on for months. So in a stroke the two people I loved most in the world betrayed me and were lost forever.

So there I was in the rainy cottage in the middle of nowhere wondering whether the sun would ever come out again when this little cat turned up on my doorstep. I found her there when I opened the door to go out and check the post. (I think I was still expecting to get a letter from one of them with an apology at that stage – very naïve of me.) There she was, this tiny cat, white all over except for some sandy splodges on her throat and two paws.

She miaowed at me and I just tried to shoo her away. But she wouldn't leave. She just went and sat on the window sill and started shouting at me through the glass. I couldn't hear her but I could see her little mouth opening.

Eventually I took pity on her and opened the door. I didn't have any cat food of course, so I gave her a tin of sardines I found in the cupboard. She wolfed that down, then came and sat on the sofa next to me while I watched whatever nonsense came on to the screen.

She leant against me and I gradually felt her warmth spreading into me. Her purring was very soothing and after a while I fell asleep.

I had these strange dreams. I was in a big, shining white room and everything was calm around me. There was a waterfall and these lovely palm trees. I suppose it was a bit like the nicest spa you've ever seen.

When I woke up the cat was still there purring next to me. I was happy where I was so I ended up bringing a pillow and blanket in from the bedroom and sleeping on the sofa with the cat.

For the next few days that was more or less the pattern of how I lived. I went to the shop every day for food, I fed the cat, and I sat on the sofa. Now and then she went outside but most of the time she spent there staring at me with these big kind eyes. I started talking to the cat, telling her about all the things that had happened to me. And then when I fell asleep I went into this strange white place where everything seemed nice and soothing. I cried a lot while I was awake, but while I was sleeping I felt like I was starting to heal.

Every day since the break up I had woken with this heavy bad feeling in my heart. On the third day that the cat was there, I woke up for the first time feeling happy. The room seemed to be full of light and I actually felt like my life might not be over after all.

That day the cat was especially affectionate. She crawled up to my shoulder and purred right in my ear and licked my face. I started to worry what I would do with her when I moved back home. And as soon as that thought struck me, she got down onto the floor and looked straight at me. I don't know why, but I was sure she knew exactly what I had thought. I said to her, "I'm going to be alright, aren't I?" It was partly a question, but also I was starting to believe it at last.

And then she went to the door and miaowed. I let her out and she gave me one last look. Then she just marched away. I saw her go through the hedge, then she walked away across the field in an absolute straight line, as though she wanted me to know she wasn't coming back.

I waited a few days to be sure. But deep down I knew that she was gone because she had done what she came to do.

Then I gathered myself together and moved home. I wasn't completely healed, but I had got through the worst of it and those few days with the cat, when I talked to her and told her all about my darkest thoughts, were the time when I had started the healing process.

Danni, 25

One of my friends was diagnosed with lymphoma in the 1990s. We were surprised because she had always been such a health freak. She religiously ate her five fruits or vegetables a day and didn't drink or smoke.

She was terrified of dying and although she didn't attend any particular church she always prayed for her friends.

As she went through treatment she became very tired and had a strange experience as she was lying in bed one day. She saw a man standing at the foot of her bed, she said that she knew that he was an angel because he had wings and looked so kind.

The angel told her not to be afraid and said that it wasn't her time yet. The next day my friend started to feel better and eventually the lymphoma had gone.

She's no longer afraid of dying. She told me that the encounter with the angel means that she knows that she will be in a lovely, peaceful place after she has died.

Frank, 24

When I was at college I developed a rather nasty case of

impetigo, which is a skin infection. The skin on my face was particularly affected – it would get all itchy and flaky and then if I touched it, it would end up becoming scabby.

This is a pretty awful thing to go through at any age, but obviously when you are a teenager you are especially sensitive to anything that affects your appearance. I became quite distraught when it wouldn't go away and started to refuse to leave my room. I hated people seeing me like that.

Realistically, my behaviour was probably prolonging the problem. I was eating badly, sleeping badly and my skin stayed in bad shape as a result. I also spent all the time on the computer playing games or surfing the internet and again this wasn't doing my health any good. It just wasn't clearing up. I seriously considered leaving college and running away to go home to my parents.

One night, I woke up and there was a woman leaning over the bed. She was older than me and looked at me like a mother or older relative would look at you – she had a very caring look in her eyes. She told me I needed to look after myself better and my skin would improve.

She put her hand on my forehead and I felt her warmth come into my skin and spread through me. She stayed there like that and I gradually fell back to sleep.

The next morning the impetigo had got ever so slightly better. I forced myself to go to the shop and buy some proper food. The next day it was better again and I felt confident enough to go out for a morning jog. The healthier I got myself the more the skin cleared up.

Finally, it was completely gone and it never got that bad again. I never saw the woman again. I suppose I might have dreamed her, but it seems to me that she was some kind of angel who took pity on me when I was at a bit of a low.

Julia, 67

My husband Peter died recently. For the last ten years of his life he suffered from Alzheimer's disease. It is a very distressing way to lose someone as they slip away from you slowly while they are still alive. It was little things he forgot at first, words, names, where things were kept. But gradually he lost more and more of his memory and ability to understand what was happening.

Even then he would have days and moments of clarity. I remember sitting crying in the kitchen once because he had been sitting looking out the window, looking confused as he often did, when he asked me if I remembered the boat trip we had taken on the River Wey. I said, "Yes," and he just sighed and said, "Wasn't that a lovely day?"

It had been a lovely day. After the trip, we had gone for a walk afterwards then had some food in a pub by the river. And that was where he asked me to marry him. So, while it was lovely that he remembered, I was also left feeling sad that the one fragment he remembered still didn't add up to the memory of the day that I cherished so much.

Eventually, I couldn't cope with him at home on my own. He was starting to be a danger to himself as he would start taps running, or turn the gas on and forget to light it. I was scared he was going to injure himself badly but I couldn't watch over him every minute of the day.

Luckily, we were able to find a care home close to where we lived. I found visiting him there dreadfully sad. I always felt that in his lucid moments he must wonder why I had abandoned him, and when he did see me he had a strange mixture of worry, shame and resentment. And even there, there would be flashes of the old Peter from time to time.

Often when I arrived to visit him, he would be walking in the garden with a younger man. This man looked to be about forty. He had a very kind, noble sort of face. I always expected him to come in and introduce himself but when I told the staff I was there and they went to fetch Peter, he would come in alone.

This went on for two years until a major stroke left Peter in a critical condition. I went to visit him once and the young man was in the corridor. He smiled at me, reassuringly as I went in to see my husband, but we didn't speak. I spent the last two hours of his life sitting there holding his hand and trying to reassure him. I don't want to talk too much about it as it was a dreadful experience.

Afterwards I left feeling numb. I drove home and tried to sleep but it was impossible. I woke at dawn and went back to the care home as there were arrangements to be made. When I got there I looked out the window to the garden where I had so often seen Peter walking with his companion. For a moment I was convinced I saw them again, walking away from the home. My heart skipped and for a moment I felt Peter was still with me and I had imagined it all. But then when I looked again I couldn't see them.

I asked the nurse who the young man was who had spent so much time with my husband. They were bewildered, had no idea what I was talking about. I described him in detail, but they just said there was no one on the staff or any of the residents that matched the description.

I believe what I saw in the garden was real and that it was the last journey of Peter's soul to another place. I like to think of him there, restored to how he was before that dreadful disease changed him. I like to imagine him on that boat on the River Wey or in the pub garden where he proposed to me, waiting patiently for me to join him again.

Isla, 52

I suffer from multiple sclerosis. I don't have it as bad as some people, but I suffer from a lot of pain, discomfort and anxiety. It is not a nice thing but it is a burden I have to carry.

I am lucky because I have a wonderful husband and family. I always make a joke with them that I don't deserve them because I'd never have been as good to them if they had been the ones who got ill, though they know that is just my sense of humour. And I'm genuinely grateful for all the people who have looked after me in good times and bad.

Sometimes when I am going through a bad patch I have a very vivid sensation of my angel being there with me. It feels like she is holding me with her arms wrapped tightly around me. If I close my eyes I can feel her and smell her and sometimes even hear her whispering in my ear. She comes when I am desperate for reassurance, for someone to lean on.

Nothing can make my problems go away altogether, but knowing she is there always makes things a bit better for me in the darkest nights.

Kenneth, 75

I've been suffering from cancer for a while. They thought they had beaten it, but it has come back and it looks like there's not much they can do this time.

I don't think I can complain too much. I have had a long life and many happy times. I didn't marry but I have a lot of nieces and nephews and several of them have children, so I had a good family around me. My main hope now is that the end isn't too painful or too soon and that I get to spend some more time with people I love.

I can be quite calm about it now, but I have to admit that

the first time I got the diagnosis I was badly upset. I was at the hospital to get the results of some tests and while they had told me they were testing for a range of possible problems I suppose I hadn't really let myself believe that it would be something serious.

I remember going outside afterwards in a bit of a daze, feeling very sorry for myself. I sat on one of the benches and looked up at the sky, wondering how I would cope. A young man came to sit next to me. He asked me if I was alright and I told him that I wasn't.

He said I could tell him about it if I wanted. And so I did. That was unusual for me because I tend to keep myself to myself. I don't like all these television programmes you get these days where people talk about all the personal things that we didn't use to mention in public. But he was very kind and listened to me. Then he sat there quietly with me for a while. I felt much better for talking to him, and when I decided it was time to move on, I thanked him for his time.

He said it was what he was there for, which I thought was a slightly odd response. I haven't seen him since, but I remember him as being either an angel or one of the kindest men I have had met.

James, 46

I had a complete meltdown when I was thirty-five. Everything in my life had been going wrong for a while. I had written a book and had it published and I had been pinning a lot of hope on it doing well. But it only sold about a hundred copies and the agent and the publisher made it clear they weren't interested in a follow-up.

That meant I was stuck in my boring life with no money again and to add to things, my girlfriend, who I had been going out with for four years, chose that moment to announce that she had decided to go back to Scandinavia on her own and she didn't want me to even think about going after her.

I know I am basically not a very nice person. I am selfish, uncaring, and slightly pathetic in general. But that doesn't mean I don't get upset by these kinds of setbacks.

However, this time, it went beyond being upset to a minor mental breakdown. I got to the point where I found it really hard to get out of bed, to wash, to go to the shop or just to function normally.

I started to wonder who I was and not to be able to remember the most basic things about myself. I would spend all day staring at a bit of dirt or fluff on the floor and wondering why people exist in the first place.

The turning point came one day when my brother called me. We don't always get on well, but he could tell immediately that I was in a bad way and invited himself round.

We spent a long time talking that night. I was pathetically grateful that he had made the effort to come and try and look after me. He slept on the floor and in the morning we talked some more.

One thing he reminded me about was the fact that I used to believe in angels. He told me that there was still an angel looking after me, even if I didn't think about it any more.

When I eventually went to bed that night I tried to open my mind, to see the world as I had when I was a child. And I had a very clear memory of the angel who used to come to look after me when I was small.

I remember the way she used to look down at me and give me strength and courage. She was there for me in some difficult times when I was a child. And seeing her face again I started to see my situation differently. I decided that night that I would try to live my life better for the angel I remembered.

Since then I have always kept her in mind, and I have tried to be less selfish and more positive in the way I approach life. I have also made friends properly with my brother – it is strange because after a long period in which we didn't get on we have started again as friends and now I really cherish his companionship.

So for me it is only a memory of an angel that changed my life. But it was a very powerful memory and it had a powerful effect in my life.

Angelic Visions

It is always fascinating to see the wide variety of ways in which angels manifest themselves in the physical world. Sometimes they come to us as friends or strangers, or even pets. Other times they come in dreams or as voices in our head. And sometimes a vision of an angel is enough to have an impact on us in our lives, whether we are in a moment of danger, decision, or simply contemplating the mysteries of life.

Carl, 42

One day, a couple of years ago, I was watching the stars out of the window when I saw a rainbow coming down towards the ground.

I went outside. It was a lovely warm night in the early autumn. Two angels appeared exactly in the place where the rainbows had been pointing.

They came towards me. There was a bright golden light coming from them. It was the most beautiful thing I had ever seen.

One of the angels came towards me. It didn't touch me, but I was enveloped in that wonderful golden light. It warmed me from top to bottom and made me feel a joy so sweet I nearly cried.

I didn't know what to say so I just looked at them, but they didn't seem to expect anything from me. After a few moments they moved away. They went back up in the direction that the rainbow had come from.

I was left with the deep, abiding belief that there are angels who visit this realm.

Zoe, 26

My mum and dad split up when I was fourteen and I blamed myself. I developed anxiety attacks and agoraphobia and became chronically depressed.

Both my parents were too wrapped up in their own

problems to see what was happening to me and I began to think seriously about taking my own life.

I remember one evening sitting on my bed wishing I could die but not having the energy to do anything about it. Suddenly, I heard a voice asking me to think about the people I would leave behind.

I then felt warmth spreading through my body from my head to my toes. I didn't see anything but I sensed that a change had come over the room. I began to cry and carried on for what felt like hours before I eventually fell asleep.

When I woke up the next morning, everything seemed better. I began reading self-help books and started keeping a diary of how I felt and what things had happened to make me feel that way.

Slowly I began to feel better and my relationship with my parents improved. It all happened years ago now and though I do still occasionally feel down I am in a much better place emotionally than I was then.

Katya, 52

I often dream about meeting angels. I find myself on a silver staircase that leads up towards the clouds. There are sparkling lights all around me, and the angels come down the stairs to meet me.

When they reach me one of them gives me a big hug. It is a lovely moment. They are full of joy, and everyone is laughing and smiling, like the best family party you ever went to.

The angels don't have wings or halos, but it is very clear who they are. They have a very strong presence and know everything about me. Sometimes they give me advice about what I should do. Sometimes they just lead me up the stairs and we go to a beautiful garden where we sit at a table on the lawn and relax.

The last time I dreamt about the angels, it was raining and the sun was shining and there was a rainbow coming down into the garden. It was an incredibly beautiful moment because I could very clearly see the rainbow reaching down to the ground.

The dream never ends there. I always have time to go back to the staircase and to walk back down to the real world.

Elizabeth, 34

When I was pregnant with my third child, I was sure that I was having a baby boy. I was very happy and could imagine myself cuddling a little boy.

When I was almost twelve weeks pregnant a scan showed that there may be problems with the baby. I was devastated and kept praying that he would be alright.

At fourteen weeks I awoke at five o'clock in the morning, with bad cramp pains in my stomach. When I went to the bathroom I was bleeding heavily so I woke my husband and asked him to take me to the hospital.

I think in my heart I knew that I had lost the baby. When I reached the hospital, tests confirmed my fears.

A few days after losing the baby, I had a dream about my grandmother who had died the year before. She told me that she would look after my baby boy and that he'd be OK.

I suddenly woke up and in the corner of the room I saw a figure, very tall and emitting a bright white light that shone into my eyes. It smiled at me and said, "Don't worry, he is safe."

Her voice was kind and gentle. Listening to her my mind began to feel at peace again and I went back to sleep. The next day I could feel my heart starting on the long road to healing.

I am comforted by the knowledge that my baby is in heaven and that I will eventually meet him.

Ben, 42

I got a fantastic job three years ago. It was my dream job really, everything I had been working towards.

The problem was that I had been so stressed in my previous job, I had been drinking too much, especially when I felt nervous or agitated. The night before I started my new job, I went to my local bar at eight o'clock, meaning to have one or two drinks, just to calm down.

Inevitably I found myself still there two hours later, getting increasingly drunk. I was telling everyone about my brilliant new job and they were buying me drinks to celebrate.

I found myself at the bar, ordering yet another beer, when a man came up to the bar next to me.

He congratulated me on my new job. Then he asked me when it started. I told him it was in the morning. He took the drink out of my hand and told me I should go home.

If anyone else had done that I would have argued with them. But there was something so calm and authoritative about this man. He said he would walk me home, and I just meekly agreed.

I left the drink behind, and followed him. He told me that for all I knew the first morning of my new job would be the most important day of my life and that I would be a fool to wreck it by turning up hungover. This was obvious advice, but I really needed someone to tell me that at that moment.

He asked me what would happen if I had to go into a meeting and introduce myself to all my colleagues after drinking too much. I admitted that I would struggle, that my hands would shake and that I would be sweaty and pale. He told me to remember that and to go inside and drink a lot of water.

By this stage we were outside my house. I remember shaking his hand and thanking him for being more sensible than me, then I went in and took his advice. A lot of water, some aspirin and a slice of toast, then I got myself into bed. In the morning I felt slightly fragile, but I was basically OK. Any more to drink and I think I would have been in a terrible state.

The reason I see all this as being something more than a kindly stranger looking out for me is what happened at work the next morning. I arrived, was shown to my new office, had a cup of tea, and was immediately called into a meeting.

It turned out that they were having the quarterly meeting, with all the most important people at the company. They had forgotten to warn me about this, but they wanted me to stand up and introduce myself to my new colleagues and the people I was overseeing.

It was a nerve-wracking moment, but it went well and set the tone for a successful year at the company. Things are still going well for me and I am drinking far less. I feel extremely lucky that I didn't manage to blow it on my very first morning by turning up with a hangover.

The fact that the very scenario the man in the bar warned me about turned out to be true was the thing I found strange. It might be a coincidence but it does feel almost as though he knew exactly what was going to happen and chose to let me know indirectly about this.

I certainly never saw him in that bar again, and it is a small local place where everyone knows everyone. I like to think he was an angel, but if he was just a kind stranger then he did me an enormous favour.

Tim, 47

I believe I saw an angel a couple of days before Christmas. It was an unusually snowy festive season and there were quite a lot of problems on the roads. I was trying to get home from work when I got stuck in a bad traffic jam.

I was concerned as to whether I was going to be able to get home. My car kept stalling and I didn't have the things I should have had like some water. I don't think I'd have been in any real danger as it was a built-up area, but I really didn't want to get stuck in the country between this town and my home town.

After a couple of hours of sitting there, I gave up and drove in towards the centre of town, where I found a motel. The car stalled just as I was trying to park and then completely died. I had to push it a few yards just to get it parked properly. I knew I was going to need a mechanic.

I was only about four miles from home but it might as well have been four hundred at that moment, with the snow still falling. I called my wife to let her know I was stuck, then went out for some dinner. To be honest I quite enjoyed the enforced peace and had some great food.

In the morning, which was Christmas Eve, I woke up really early. The light was that strange yellow-grey colour you get when there is snow on the ground. On the spur of the moment I decided that my car could stay where it was until after the holiday. It was safely parked, and I didn't like the idea of waiting around for a mechanic to mend it.

I wasn't completely sure I'd be able to walk home as the snow was pretty deep, but I decided to give it a go. It seemed safer to try now than it would have been in the dark the night before. I walked out of the town centre and found the small country road that leads to where we live. The snow was banked high on the verges but there were tyre tracks down the middle which seemed OK to walk on.

I was pleased I had decided to walk. It was incredibly beautiful and quiet out there. The only sound was the icy crunching under my feet. Snow covered everything, including the hedgerows and the trees and barns. At that time of day there was no traffic and it felt wonderfully Christmassy.

The road passes by a low hill near to the town. That was where I saw the angel. She was just standing on the hillside looking down over the town beyond. She was about 100 yards away from me, but I saw her quite distinctly, with the faint outline of wings to her side. It seemed like she was watching over the town and the people there.

Then I slipped and nearly fell. When I managed to right myself I realised she was no longer there. Either she had moved away at great speed or simply disappeared.

I've always believed in angels, and I am just glad that I got to see one, and in such peaceful and pleasant circumstances rather than in a moment of crisis.

Cally, 54

I have this repetitive dream about my father.

I am walking along a river path. It is quite a treacherous path, quite muddy, with sandy parts that slope towards the river. In these parts it is hard to keep my feet. But the river is beautiful, with reeds in the water and willows overhanging the water.

At a certain point while I am struggling along this path, I look across the water. And I see my father walking in a lovely meadow on the other side.

He is always there with an angel. I can't tell you how I know it is an angel. It is just clear from the way he stands and walks, from how magnificent he looks and his expression. He walks with my father and they seem to be talking quietly and calmly to each other.

I always try to call to my father, as I would love to talk to him. (He died fifteen years ago and I miss him every day.)

It is very difficult to shout in a dream and I find I don't have a voice. Mostly I wake up at this point, feeling frustrated. But on a few occasions I have managed to call to him.

When that has happened, he has turned towards me and given me a lovely smile of recognition. Then he and the angel wave to me.

I always want to jump into the water and swim across to talk to him. But at the same time I know that my place is here on this muddy, rocky path and that when the time comes for me to cross the river and be with him it will happen naturally.

David, 23

My uncle, my mom's brother died about four weeks ago. My mom was very upset because she had been very close to him. They were only a year apart in age and he was only forty-two. When he died his wife telephoned us a few hours later to give us the sad news.

I drove to the hospital with my mom and we were shown into a little room where my uncle's body was lying. My mom kissed his forehead and held his hand. It was really hard to believe that he had died and we'd never see him again.

After the funeral we had some people back to our house and my mom made everybody some tea. My mom and her other sister sat and talked about my uncle and the fun times they that had had. We had lit candles for my uncle and as the evening wore on the flames seemed to be blowing around as if there were drafts in the room, but there weren't.

My mom told me that after everyone had left and I'd gone up to bed she was putting the candles out so that she could come to bed herself and there was one candle that wouldn't be extinguished. She said it made her laugh, like one of those joke candles. When she finally managed to extinguish it she heard a voice beside her very clearly.

"He's alright," it said. She looked round but there was no one there. We believe that it was an angel come to reassure and comfort her.

Krystyna, 38

I love to walk in my local graveyard. It is a beautiful place with an old chapel at the centre, a lot of interesting statues like stone angels and animals and winding paths that go through the trees. I find it soothing to wander around there when I have things to think about.

The paths are quite long and you can see a long way down them. Several times I have had the feeling that I saw an angel. Once I distinctly saw a woman in white walking behind an old couple. As I got nearer to them, she was no longer there and I could only see the couple. They had deeply sad expressions on their faces and I couldn't help but wonder whether they had been visiting the grave of a loved one who had recently passed on.

Another time, when I was there early in the morning, I saw a shimmering shape hovering near the chapel. It seemed to resolve itself into a human shape, and then a man who walked into the chapel. I walked all the way up the path to try and see what had happened. I followed him into the chapel, but there was no one inside.

Holly, 40

I didn't believe in angels or in any kind of supernatural or spiritual reality until I came close to death. What I know now is that I had a blood clot and it gummed up my blood vessels. The doctors told me that after the event. All I knew at the time was that started to feel terrible and came over very faint and everything started to go black. I apparently lost consciousness and my boyfriend called an ambulance.

I woke up on a trolley in the emergency room, with people in white coats and nurses all around me. Then I faded out and find myself flying out of my body. I found that I was in the same room, but looking down on my own body. The doctors and nurses were working away, pumping at my chest, and they were bringing some machinery. But I just lost interest and left the room. I floated along the corridor.

Since I could fly, I decided that the most interesting thing to do would be to fly up over the city, so I did. It was very beautiful. I could see the hospital and beyond that the lights of the business district.

Then I looked up and instead of the starry sky I was expecting, the whole sky above me was a wash of white light. I was ecstatic and knew that all I wanted was to go up into the light.

However, someone took me by the arm and started to pull me down. I looked around and saw that an angel was there next to me. She didn't have wings, but I knew she was an angel because she had a face that was beautiful and wise but ancient at the same time.

I told her I wanted to go up to the light but she told me it wasn't time yet. She said that when the time came the light would still be there, but that I still had things to do in the human world. I particularly remember that phrase because that was what made me sure she came from beyond the human world and was an angel.

She dragged me all the way down from that beautiful sky, through a window of the hospital, back down the same hospital, and then suddenly I was back there on the same trolley gasping and looking up into the faces of the doctor who was working on me.

My immediate reaction was one of great sorrow. I had wanted to go to the light. But then once I had time to get over what had happened I was so pleased to be alive. I realised the angel had been right and that it would have been too soon to leave. Now that I have seen the light though, I am not at all scared of dying. I know that when my time comes I will be going back to that wonderful light and that I will be happy, not sad to see it again.

Colin, 72

I often feel the presence of angels when I am in the church.

I go most mornings for a moment of peace and prayer. I find it very peaceful and soothing. My health isn't so good these days and I can't kneel to pray, but I sit down and have a moment of calm.

I see the angels at the altar, great shining beings who are from somewhere else altogether. I don't know if I have lived a good enough life to expect to go to heaven, but I find seeing them very reassuring. I don't know if I have weeks, months or even years to live, but I hope that when I do die I will get to talk to them and find out more the mysteries of this world and the next.

Tariq, 45

When I was younger I was in the Iranian army, during the war with Iraq. I didn't have much choice about it, and it was one of the reasons I ended up leaving my homeland to live abroad. It was a terrible time and I was injured when a shell exploded close to me – there were many who were less lucky than me. I was only hit in the leg by shrapnel and the medics were able to do a good job so that today I just have a slight limp. Many of those who were there at the same time died, lost limbs, were blinded or were gassed. I'm told that the nearest equivalent to the fighting in that war, was World War One – in the same way we spent a lot of time digging trenches and fighting for weeks to win half a mile of ground only to lose it again the next month. And it was all in the service of leaders who were deranged in their ideas and intentions.

I remember as I was being taken on a stretcher away

from the scene for medical attention, I looked up at the clouds. I distinctly saw the shapes of three angels looking down at the battlefield. One had a very stern face and was pointing at the ground. One had a very beautiful face but it was turned away from us and toward the sky. While the third angel looked down on us and wept.

I believe that any time that foolish leaders send men to die and mutilate one another the angels will be there to show their pity, their rage and their sorrow for mankind. I wish I could believe that we would learn not to behave in this way, but sadly we don't seem to want to follow the path of the angels in the world today.

Albert, 47

I had a strange vision of some angels one time when I was out for a long walk in the Peak District.

I was high up a hill above the lowlands, a long way from any town or village. Even the nearest farmhouse must have been a few miles away, down below me.

As I was walking I had been thinking about my faith in God, and what I believed in. I had been thinking about all the terrible things that happen in the world, the cruelty, wars, religious intolerance and hatred that seems to define the world.

I suppose I was wondering whether a world where such awful things happen can possibly be a world that was created by God.

I sat down and looked up at the sky above me. I remember asking God whether he was there, and why the world was such an unkind, graceless place.

As I stared up, three angels appeared above me. They were awe-inspiring, shining creatures, hovering in the air above the landscape. They didn't speak, but they looked down at me and held their hands out as though in greeting.

I stared at them in wonder for a few moments, and then just as they had appeared out of nothing, they disappeared again.

I am not sure why they appeared at that moment. You could say it was to reassure me that there really is an angelic realm when I was experiencing a moment of doubt. After all, it would be pretty unlikely that God would himself come to speak to me, but perhaps it is more likely that angels would respond to a human in a moment of need.

I found it inspiring, though. It made me think harder about what I had been asking of God and to see that I was being self-indulgent.

I always go back to the bible when I am suffering from doubt, and I take seriously the idea that God has given us free will. So the terrible things that happen are our own choices. But also I must remember that every day millions of people make wise, good, kind choices in their lives.

The world is a place of great good as well as great evil. It is up to us which choices we make in life. We might have God or the angels to help us, but we can't know for sure. But that doesn't mean we can't take responsibility for our own choices and decisions.

Miscellany

Some of the accounts of angels I received for this book aren't easy to categorise into any of the other sections. So in this final section I have gathered together a variety of these accounts, which I didn't want to leave out simply because they were a little different or unusual.

Carl, 28

This is a bit of a silly story, but I will tell you it and let you make your own minds up.

I got married last year. I had the stag night a week before the wedding (I'm not stupid enough to do it the night before…) Predictably, I got very drunk and my friends thought it would be funny to play a trick on me.

They took me to a traffic island in the middle of a busy roundabout near to where we live and left me there in my underpants, handcuffed to a tree.

I woke up sometime around dawn. It wasn't that cold as it was right in the warmest period of the summer, but I was a bit damp and uncomfortable, as well as extremely confused and hungover. Basically I had no idea where I was but I was attached to this tree and feeling sick and ill.

I managed to get myself free (by breaking a branch). Then I had to work out to get to safety. This is the moment when I was in some genuine danger. The morning rush hour was just starting – they had presumably left me there at the dead of night when it was easy to get to the island, but now I was stranded with really busy traffic streaming past me. I was cursing my friends, but I had to get away somewhere.

I had a go at getting across the road and nearly died. A car came round the corner far faster than I had imagined it would and I had to leap back to the grass behind me, with horns honking everywhere. It wasn't at all funny even if it sounds like it might have been a funny sight.

Then a man walked across the traffic island from behind me. I say that simply, but it was an extraordinary thing to see him there. I had no idea where he had come from or how he had reached the island. He was well dressed, in a nice suit. He reached down and took my hand and then led me to the other side of the island. He simply led me out into the traffic, holding up his hand and, amazingly, the oncoming cars obeyed him. They stopped and allowed us to walk steadily across the road, without any horns or abuse. It was a weird moment of peace in the midst of chaos.

Then, as soon as we were on the other side, the traffic all roared off again. The moment of peace was over. The man kept his hand on my shoulder until I was on the pavement. Then he smiled at me, shook my hand, turned around and set off down the road.

Whoever he was, he helped me when I was in trouble, in danger and in a state of serious humiliation. Maybe it is silly to call him an angel, and actually I don't mean to say I literally think he was an angel.

However, the way I see it, sometimes in life you find people who help you out at the moment of greatest need. They may not actually be angels, but they are nonetheless doing the work of the angels.

From that ludicrous moment I have personally taken real inspiration. Since then I have found myself in situations a few times where I could be the one who could play the role of the angel's helper. One time I found an old man face down on the pavement late at night and, instead of just walking by and assuming he was a drunk, I stopped to see if he needed help. And it turned out he wasn't drunk at all, but had had a fit and needed medical help.

Another time, I lent a young woman enough money to get a taxi home when she was being harassed by an aggressive man late at night in the city – I never got the money back, I didn't ask her to repay it or give her any contact details. I just took pleasure in knowing I had been able to help someone out when they needed it. She had been quite scared and was extremely grateful that I helped her. The man was angry and I had to make a swift retreat, but I came to no harm.

I like to imagine that angels will help us sometimes. But I think it probably makes them happier when we manage to help each other without any need for them to intervene.

Graham, 23

My granddad told me that he sees spirits all the time. He lives with grandma in a house that was built in the 1950s. The house was brand new when they moved in and apart from my mum they are the only people ever to have lived there. Granddad told me that there is a man in a fedora hat who smiles from the hallway whenever he watches television. Apparently this man likes it when my granddad watches cowboy films. My grandma often grumbles that he's talking rubbish because she has never seen anyone in the house but he insists that the man is there.

Another time, my granddad said that when he was a teenager he saw his next door neighbour, Vera Pilkington, come out of her front door and start walking down the street. She was walking beside a tall woman in a white dress who had her arm around her shoulders.

He said that he wanted to get her attention because she always gave him soda bottles to cash in for money at the shop, so he ran down the street shouting, "Mrs Pilkington, Mrs Pilkington!" He said that he chased her for quite a while but she never turned around,

He went to Vera's house and her husband opened the door. His eyes were red with crying and he was clearly very upset. When my granddad told him that he had been chasing Mrs Pilkington down the street to ask if he had any soda bottles her husband went pale. He told my granddad that he had just got a call from the hospital to say his wife had just died. My granddad believes that Mrs Pilkington had gone home to say her goodbyes before she left for the spirit world.

Yolande, 52

Where I live I look out over a nursery school. At lunchtimes and sometimes at the end of the day all the little children come out to play on the grass. I love watching them. It is like seeing a lot of little kittens or puppies playing around, chasing each other, falling over and getting up again. It is the sweetest thing.

Several times I have seen an angel watching them, too. The angel stands on the far side of the play area, where she can see all the children. It seems obvious to me that it is a place that an angel would want to be – if their job is to watch over innocent souls then where better could they choose?

The angel stands very still. If you have ever seen a heron standing by a pond, you'll know that they are very good at being motionless. That is how the angel is, though I imagine her eyes are busy taking in everything. If I hadn't once chanced to see her, then I don't suppose I would even notice her. But now I know she is likely to be there I find that if I look very closely I often see her.

Jo, 45

My grandmother died from liver disease many years ago. I couldn't go to her funeral as I was living overseas at the time. I had been very close to her when I was a little girl but hadn't stayed in close contact as I'd grown older. Many years later, (about two years ago), my father died from cancer. I was still overseas but managed to get time off to come home and look after him during his final days.

When he eventually died I had a strange dream that was set in a cemetery. There was a plaid blanket by an open grave and my grandmother was sitting there with my cousin Sally. She smiled at both of us and said that she wished us well in life and told us that she was always looking over us. I was confused that Sally was in the dream because I'd hardly seen her since we were kids and certainly never thought about her. Then my grandmother turned to walk away. There was an angel standing beyond the grave and she took her hand – they walked off together.

The strangest thing is that when we got to the cemetery the next morning, it was exactly the same as the cemetery in my dream. I'd never been there before but everything was identical. I also got a shock when I saw my cousin Sally. She'd broken her legs in a car accident and was being pushed in a wheelchair by her dad, my Uncle John. Across her lap was the same plaid blanket that I'd seen in my dream.

Later, I told her about my dream and she told me that she had had a very similar dream set in the same cemetery. It turned out that Sally and I were the only two people at my dad's funeral who hadn't been to our grandmother's funeral. We're now sure that she was trying to talk to us from beyond the grave and we have kept in much better touch with each other since. I think the spiritual encounter has brought us closer together.

Caroline, 18

When I was eight years old my little sister, who was just three at the time, died. Ever since then she has communicated with her whole family in various different forms. Not long after her death I was asleep with my mother, in her bed, (I was afraid to sleep alone for a while as my sister and I had always shared a room), when I noticed two shadowy figures standing in the corner of the room. I wasn't frightened because a little voice was saying in my head, "It's alright, there's nothing to worry about." The shapes gradually took on the appearance of an angel and my three-year-old sister, smiling and waving at me. I think they came to tell me that they were OK and the angel was looking after my baby sister.

On many other occasions my sister has contacted me and clearly wanted to play. I have had my hair pulled many times, just gently not aggressively, and I've heard quiet giggling coming from the wardrobe. When this happens I often open the door and say "Found you!" as if we were playing hide and seek. My mother has also found my sister's dolls in the kitchen cupboards and my laptop sometimes boots up in the middle of the night when it's switched off.

When I feel sad I always feel her presence around me. During these occasions she doesn't pull my hair or try to make me play, she just sits with me, being a companion. The whole family is convinced that my sister is around us all the time and we are grateful for that.

Cassandra, 29

When I was in my early twenties I was in a very abusive relationship. Friends and family told me to get out of it but I couldn't. I had no self-esteem and we had a baby boy.

One evening, we were having a fight and I told him to leave because my baby was asleep in the next room. My boyfriend went to his car and came back with a gun. He pointed the gun at me then fired.

I saw the flash from the gun but I didn't hear anything. Something brushed against my arm and then I saw the bullet hit the opposite wall.

My boyfriend ran out of the house thinking that he had just shot me and I stared at the wall in front of me in amazement. Something had caught the bullet in mid-air and had thrown it at the wall to stop it hitting me.

Quickly, I rushed into the other room to make sure my baby was alright and I saw an angel standing over her crib. He smiled at me and touched the baby's forehead then vanished.

I think that day I saw my guardian angel and I know now that he is protecting me and my baby. I am now much braver and I don't have anything to do with my baby's father but my family and friends help me out a lot.

Keith, 54

For some reason, I find that when I am driving in my car I sometimes feel like I am in touch with an angel. It is like a voice in my head that I can't always hear, and something about the focused but calm state you get into when driving encourages me to be able to hear it more clearly. (I should explain I live out in a backwoods part of the country and when I drive I can often go for an hour without seeing more than two or three other vehicles. I don't seriously believe that I would be in that kind of calm, meditative mood if I were driving in a big city!)

We talk about the things in my life that are worrying me, the problems facing my children, issues in my marriage. All kinds of things, the subjects you would talk about to your best friend or maybe to a priest if you were in an organised religion. (I have a faith in some kind of God but I am not sure that any of the existing religions should be treated as being the one and only truth. To me it makes more sense to read religious texts and to see that many of them have certain principles of kindness, empathy and humanity in common.)

It feels as though the angel is sitting in the seat next to me and, while I can't see them, I have a strong sense of a presence in the car. Sometimes we don't even talk. I can drive for hours just feeling that sense that I am not alone and that if I need help or advice there is always someone I can turn to.

Colin, 46

My aunt Sally used to keep doves in her back garden. She had a dovecote and she would be out there a lot, talking to them and feeding them. She loved them as pets.

After she died, one of her friends took her doves and looked after them, which was lucky as no one in the family knew much about how to care for them. At her funeral, just as the coffin was going in to be cremated, I looked out of the window of the chapel and I saw two white doves sitting on a wall looking at the church.

Since then I have see the same thing on a few occasions. Once, when we finally sold Sally's house I came out of it for the last time and saw two doves sitting on the chimney. They looked down and then flew off.

Another time I saw them sitting on a telephone line. It could of course be a coincidence. But the fact that the first time I saw those two doves was at her funeral makes me feel that their appearances are in some way connected to my aunt. The white feathers always make me think of angels, and I hope that wherever she is Sally is happy with her doves.

Jo, 21

When he was younger, my father worked in Germany. One night after he'd been out with friends he decided to walk home because he didn't have very much money and it was only a couple of miles. He lived in a residential area on the edge of town and the quickest way to get there was down an unpaved, dirt road.

As he was walking down this road a car driving past him in the opposite direction did a u-turn and started to follow him. Looking behind him he saw that there were four men in the car and they looked quite dangerous. The rest of the road was deserted, no people, no cars. Afraid for his safety he stepped into the undergrowth at the side of the road and broke into a run. The car just followed him.

Suddenly as if from nowhere another car came along in the opposite direction and this also did a u-turn and drove up beside him. At first he was afraid that it was some kind of criminal ambush but this car was being driven by a man who rolled down the window and told him to get in. My father told me that when he looked into the man's face he felt so safe.

The man had really kind eyes and my father got into the car without hesitating. The man asked him for his address and drove him home. They didn't talk much because my dad wasn't that fluent in German at the time and the man spoke only basic English.

When he got home my father walked up to his apartment block and turned to wave goodbye but the car had vanished. My father didn't hear the engine and from when he'd got out of the car the whole street had been silent. If the car had driven off he would have heard it.

The next day the newspapers carried photographs of four men they wanted to question about several violent robberies, two of which had left men dead. The pictures were of the men that my father had seen following him the night before. He believes that the man driving the car was his guardian angel and without him he may have been killed that night.

Jenny, 33

I've always been convinced that I'm very sensitive to the spirit world and so more receptive to conversing with the dead than most people. I've had quite a few experiences in my life, mostly involving family members who have passed over. One experience happened in California, in the summer of 1999. I was living in a small apartment there, in an older building, where I often had the feeling that someone was watching me.

One night I suddenly woke up at 3.00 am and could see a white mist at the foot of the bed. I wasn't scared and my only thought at the time was irritation that I was being woken from a good night's sleep. I decided to go and sleep on the sofa, mad I know, but all I wanted to do was go back to sleep.

Seconds later, someone tapped me on the shoulder. When I turned round, however, no one was there. I tried to go back to sleep and was drifting off when I felt another tap on my shoulder. I shouted into the room, telling whoever it was that I needed to get some sleep because I had work tomorrow. At that moment I heard a voice saying "Jenny, no it's me, Jon." This startled me awake because I've always been close to my kid brother.

I asked what the matter was and he told me that he was in the hospital but wouldn't be there for long. He said he had to go and wanted to say goodbye. He also told me that our angel was there with him.

This scared me because when we were kids we used to talk about our guardian angel. When he was doing something silly like climbing a tree too high he would make a joke about how he hoped the guardian angel was ready for him. My mum told us we had a guardian angel but I thought that just ended up encouraging him to take risks he might not have otherwise. By this time, I couldn't have got to sleep any more and was up and about feeling scared.

I called the local hospital and the ER staff told me that a young man with the name of Jon had been brought in during the early hours of the morning. He had been stabbed by a gang whilst trying to protect an elderly man who was being attacked by the gang, probably for his wallet. My brother had died at 3.00 am.

Joan, 49

My daughter Susie was in a nasty car accident a few years ago. Fortunately her two children weren't with her at the time.

Susie had dropped the children off at day-care and then set out to do her usual weekly shop at a nearby town. She told me later that as she pulled away from the kerb after dropping off the children she heard a woman's voice telling her to put her seatbelt on. She never puts it on and I've warned her about it for years, but she told me that the voice was so unexpected that she followed the advice and put on her seatbelt.

As she steered around a corner on the main road her car hit a patch of black ice and the car went skidding on to some railings at the side of the road. The railings pierced the car through the windscreen. Susie had some quite serious internal injuries. But she didn't get thrown forward on to the railings and that would most probably have been fatal. That is what would have happened if she hadn't been wearing her seatbelt.

I got a call from the hospital letting me know what had happened. I immediately jumped into the car and set off for the hospital. As I drove I was shaking but I kept hearing a woman's voice telling me that Susie was going to be OK.

It took a while, but Susie did make a good recovery. Later on, she described what had happened. She also told me about a kind, calm woman's voice that had kept her going when she was in the ambulance.

I am convinced that my Susie was helped by an angel that night and that the same angel came to comfort me as I waited for Susie's recovery.

Bethany, 24

When I was in college one of my friends bought a Ouija board and we arranged to have a gathering in her room to try it out. We lit a circle of candles and put out the lights the sat on floor in a circle around the board. Someone invited the sprits to contact us and the planchette started moving. We were all arguing about whether or not someone was pushing it but everyone denied doing so. It moved to "Yes" to indicate that there was a spirit who wanted to communicate with us.

My older sister had run away from home two years previously and had never contacted our family again; I really missed her and wished she would get in touch. She had left at the age of eighteen to be with her boyfriend who my parents didn't like and tried to stop her seeing. I asked the board of it knew where my sister was and it pointed to "Yes."

At this point I was absolutely fascinated and wanted to ask more questions. But I suddenly saw an angel standing on the far side of the room. It was staring at me and shaking its head.

I suddenly had a real sense of dread about what we were doing. I tried to persuade my friends to stop playing with board but they wouldn't. Even though I was desperate to know what had happened to my sister, I just stood up and walked out of the room.

I saw my friends the next day and they told me things had got a bit strange after I left. None of them seemed to have enjoyed the experience. In fact, I would say that they seemed quite nervous, as though they felt they had been in touch with evil spirits.

A few days later, my sister finally got back in touch with us. She told me that had had a dream in which an angel told her I wanted to know how she was.

Josie, 26

My mother died when I was six years old and I don't remember her very well. I do remember that at the time of her death I didn't understand what had happened and just wanted to see her. I was brought up by her sister, my Auntie Emily who was kind and had no children of her own, but I still missed having a mother like other children had.

One day when I was about nine, we were at a coffee shop and my Auntie Emily had gone to use the bathroom. A young woman came in and came over to our table where I was waiting alone. She seemed to know me and was asking all about how I was and what I was doing at school. Then she told me that she would never leave my side, even though sometimes I wouldn't be able to see her.

When my Auntie Emily returned from the bathroom I told her about the lady and described her. Back at her house later, she showed me an old photograph album with a picture of my mother in it when she was about twenty. It was the exact same woman that came to talk to me in the coffee shop.

I hadn't recognised her because I remembered her looking very different when she was older. I know now that my mother is my guardian angel and I believe that she will walk through my life by my side.

Holly, 27

When I was a teenager there was a series of rapes and murders in our area. We all knew about them and all the grown-ups kept telling us to be careful, but of course I was only a kid and I thought it would never happen to me.

One night I was waiting for my dad to pick me up after work. I washed dishes in a local restaurant and this was after the evening shift. I decided to start walking down the road, so I could surprise him by flagging him down on the way. But about a hundred yards down the road, this car came round the corner and started crawling alongside me. I immediately regretted walking on my own, but there was not much I could do.

The car pulled up just beside me and a man got out with a baseball cap pulled down over his head and his hands hidden inside his jacket. I was terrified and just started to run. It was a deserted road and there was no way I could get away from him, but I thought I might be able to hide somehow.

He didn't get back in the car, he just ran after me. I am pretty fast but he was gaining on me. And then I tripped and fell down. I grazed my knees really painfully and smacked my elbow on the concrete then rolled over. His feet slowed down behind me and he came and stood over me as I lay on my side. I didn't try to get up, but even though I was a bit dazed I was wondering hopelessly if I could maybe bite him or hurt him somehow if he tried to touch me. I was feeling a little desperate.

I don't really know what happened after that. There was a kind of flash of white light and he looked up at something behind me. It seemed like it was giving off a strong light. He just looked terrified and turned and ran away. He got into his car and drove off at speed in the opposite direction.

The light only lasted for a few seconds and when I rolled on to my back I couldn't see anything. Painfully I got myself on to my feet. My knee was bleeding and my elbow hurt badly, but nothing was broken. I started to limp in the direction of my house. A few moments later my dad's car came along. I waved him down, and he was shocked by how I looked.

He was obviously worried and upset, though of course his first reaction was to shout at me for being so incredibly foolish. But he calmed down right away, got me in the car and took me home and everyone fussed over me. They got the police round to hear my story, but I didn't tell them the bit about the flash of light, just that he had run off for some reason.

I've no idea what really happened. But I do wonder if it might have been an angel that saved me. After that day we didn't hear about any more deaths in the area, so perhaps the killer either stopped or moved away.

Dora, 58

After my mother died I was going through a really bad time, crying a lot and feeling really lacking in energy and enthusiasm for anything. One day as I sat on the sofa feeling very depressed, I felt a presence near me in the room. It was calm and comforting like when my mother used to hug me. A figure began to materialise in front of me.

It was a tall man with grey hair and very striking, kind blue eyes. He was very colourfully dressed. The colours almost didn't seem like the colours we have in our world. I got the feeling that he was telling me that he was from the transient world between Earth and Heaven.

He leaned down towards me and smiled. He asked me if I had a question for him and I asked him how my mother was doing. He told me that she was doing just fine and would probably contact me when she was settled in Heaven. I thanked him for coming to see me and he slowly vanished. When I came back to reality I felt on top of the world. I was so thankful for the amazing gift that he had given me. The best comfort I could wish for in my time of need.

I know he was a guiding angel who helps us make the transition between life and death. He was so gentle and emanated so much love that I have no fear of death now. I know I will be with my mother and that there are kind wonderful beings on the other side who sometimes visit us on this side.

Len, 67

My wife, Jenny, died from breast cancer last year. We had been together for twenty-five years. The day she died I was in the bedroom with her and working on my laptop because I had work to do but I didn't want to leave her. I could tell from her breathing that she wouldn't be alive much longer.

Suddenly my computer crashed and then a weird image began floating across the screen. I looked up and my wife had passed away. The computer had the strange image on it for the next few hours, whilst I telephoned the doctor and our relatives to give them the news.

That night I restarted the computer and it was fine. However, the day of her funeral the same thing happened again. I think that it was angels causing the computer to go funny. Firstly to get my attention as my wife died and then to let me know that she is now at peace and free from pain.

Katherine, 28

Many years ago I was going through a very sad time; I always felt very lonely even when other people were around me. Suddenly, my mom announced that she was pregnant.

It was, for her, a very late baby - she was forty-six. Tests apparently confirmed that her baby might have a serious heart condition. We were all really anxious about this news because we didn't know anything about the illness or how we'd cope.

Late one night, I was lying in bed thinking things over when I saw a movement out of the corner of my eye. There was a little boy standing in the hallway. I went to the door and he held out his hand. When I took it he looked into my eyes and smiled. His face was so wise and gentle. From then on I knew that everything would be OK.

The next morning, I mentioned this incident to Mom and she said it was weird because she had also been "dreaming" of a boy with an angel face. My baby brother was born two months later.

He was perfectly healthy and we were all so thankful to God. The strange thing is, as he grew up he started to look more and more like the angel boy that I saw that night. He is still the baby of the family and his nickname is "Angel."